COMMUNICATION @ WORK

How to Use Behaviour Analysis for Business Success

ALLY YATES

JAICO PUBLISHING HOUSE
Ahmedabad Bangalore Bhopal Bhubaneswar Chennai
Delhi Hyderabad Kolkata Lucknow Mumbai

Published by Jaico Publishing House
A-2 Jash Chambers, 7-A Sir Phirozshah Mehta Road
Fort, Mumbai - 400 001
jaicopub@jaicobooks.com
www.jaicobooks.com

© Ally Yates

First published in the United Kingdom in 2017 by
Panoma Press Ltd.
48 St. Vincent Drive, St. Albans
Hertfordshire AL1 5SJ, UK

To be sold only in India, Bangladesh, Bhutan,
Pakistan, Nepal, Sri Lanka and the Maldives.

MASTER COMMUNICATION@WORK
ISBN 978-93-88423-51-9

Original English language edition published as
Utter Confidence

First Jaico Impression: 2019

No part of this book may be reproduced or utilized in
any form or by any means, electronic or
mechanical including photocopying, recording or by any
information storage and retrieval system,
without permission in writing from the publishers.

Printed by
Rashmi Graphics, Mumbai

Dedication

To my sisters, Chrisi and Winnie, for helping me to work

To my boys, George, Harry and Fin, for inspiring me with your resourcefulness

To my husband, Karl, for your challenge, support and love

Acknowledgements

This book has been inspired by the pioneers of Behaviour Analysis, most notably Neil Rackham and Peter Honey. Their work in the early 1970s taught me so much about behavioural skill and training design that has enriched my work.

I am indebted to colleagues from my time at Huthwaite Research Group, in particular Linda Marsh, Andy Blanchard, Robbie Macpherson and Tony Hipgrave, for their collaboration on Behaviour Analysis research and training. I also wish to acknowledge my colleague, mentor and friend, Hank Williams, who has contributed to my thinking about Behaviour Analysis and to my development as a facilitator, consultant and coach.

Special thanks go to Patricia Riddell, Professor of Applied Neuroscience at Reading University, who has deepened my enthusiasm for and understanding of neuroscience and whose teaching has helped me to see the connections between brain and behaviour.

An outstanding group of people gave their time and helpful critique to shape the writing of this book. Thank you for your generosity and for your thoughtful and welcome guidance, which I hope you will see reflected in this final text.

Importantly, my thanks go to my clients, many of whom have been co-creating with me since I first became an independent consultant and whose stories feature in the following pages, albeit with pseudonyms. You know the power of Behaviour Analysis and I am humbled by the changes you have made. In particular I want to acknowledge James Evans who has been unstinting in encouraging me to write this book.

I give special thanks to the team of Behaviour Analysts who do great work with clients, providing insights and shaping behaviour for both teams and individuals.

And on a personal note, I thank my family for sharing the (happy) burden that writing a book brings and tolerating my absence with warmth and humour. I hope that you have utter confidence in all that you do.

Ally Yates

"Day by day, what you do is
who you become…"

Heraclitus

CONTENTS

Acknowledgements 4

FOREWORD 8

   1   Let Me Tell You A Secret... 11

   2   Using Behavioural Analysis 29

   3   Making Meetings Effective 43

   4   Establishing Your Presence 67

   5   Fostering Creativity 81

   6   Reacting 93

   7   Expressing Feelings 113

   8   Influencing Others 123

   9   Behaviour Analysis in Virtual Teams 141

   10 Putting Behaviour Analysis into Practice 151

References 167

Appendix A 172

Appendix B 174

Appendix C 175

About the Author 178

FOREWORD by Professor Neil Rackham

When Peter Honey and I developed our original Behaviour Analysis method in the early 1970s our aim was to create tools that let researchers, educators and consultants analyse what was going on during team and group meetings. It wasn't just intellectual curiosity that drove us, it was the pressing problem of how to make teams more effective.

Others had developed behaviour analysis instruments before us, notably Robert Bales, who created the granddaddy of instruments in 1950. He called it the Interaction Process Analysis, otherwise known as IPA, and it is still used by researchers today. So the idea of dividing behaviour into categories and counting their frequency wasn't a new one. There had been active research using Bales for more than 20 years before Peter and I came on the scene.

We didn't set out to create anything new. At first we thought we could use the Bales IPA. But we found it had a number of crippling disadvantages. Two of these were showstoppers. Firstly, Bales was difficult to use: it sometimes took several months of training before an analyst learned to code behaviour accurately. We needed something that could be used by practical trainers and business coaches. Months were out of the question – we were lucky to get three days to develop coding skills.

The second disadvantage was even more serious. Bales used categories like "**Negative Socio-emotional Behaviour**". Even to professional psychologists like Peter and myself, it was hard to know what some of these categories meant – one reason why it took people weeks or months to learn the IPA. We were developing a practical tool, so we needed simple, natural language terms for the behaviours we measured.

The resulting instruments, and their many variants, have been widely used to coach and train teams in many of the world's leading companies. Consulting companies like Huthwaite International have built on the original work and there has been a small but enthusiastic group of individuals, like Ally, who have made Behaviour Analysis into powerful tools for improving team and personal effectiveness.

Curiously, even though the methods we developed are now over 40 years old, they are going through a dramatic renaissance. Teamwork has replaced the old command and control structures of companies. Increasingly, students work in teams. The sad fact is, the world is not very good at analysing and developing team skills. So Behaviour Analysis is coming into its own.

That's fantastic news for me. I've been able to go back as visiting professor to my old psychology department at Sheffield University, where all this started, to work on the next generation of behaviour analysis methods with the talented research team of Professor Rod Nicolson, Professor Jeremy Dawson, Dr Sam Farley and Rose Evison. I'm particularly pleased to be working with Rose as she and I developed many of the original ideas together before she took the methods into her counselling research.

And now to Ally Yates' book and why I think it's such a valuable contribution. The theory of Behaviour Analysis is well documented. What's less understood, and equally important, is how to turn that theory into practice. Ally uses real examples, case studies and stories to show what a dramatic difference these methods can make to organisations and the individuals who work in them. In doing so she brings the methods alive. She answers the question that I find hardest to handle: "How does counting the number of behaviours used by members of a team transform team effectiveness?" Read her book and you'll understand.

Professor Neil Rackham
Sheffield University

CHAPTER 1

Let Me Tell You A Secret...

"The more we share, the more we have."

Leonard Nimoy

In this book, I'm going to share with you one of the best-kept secrets in personal development: a simple yet remarkably effective tool that has transformed the performance of individuals and teams across geographies and market sectors. Since the late 1980s, I've been helping individuals, groups and teams become more effective in their interactions at work by using a tool known as Behaviour Analysis.

Business thrives on interaction, whether we're at meetings, making presentations, coaching, or simply chatting with colleagues. Our work is increasingly team-based, a point underlined by a recent Harvard study which found collaborative activities making up more than 50% of work in business environments. There's good reason for this, since teams and groups achieve better results than the lone genius (see James Surowiecki: *The Wisdom of Crowds*). Outside the world of work, team-focused learning is increasingly taking hold as the organisational model for universities, requiring students to better understand their own behaviours as well as those of their peers.

I'd argue that how you behave in these interactions is a major contributor to your success. Indeed, your ability to work effectively with colleagues can be a source of competitive advantage for your team and your business. There's a strong case for the view that the *behavioural dimensions* of work – the 'how' rather than the 'what' – exert the biggest influence on success or failure. For example:

- 57% of IT projects fail because of breakdowns in communications

- successive change initiatives fail to gain traction (despite a compelling vision) because people stick with what they know

- on average we spend 6.5 hours a day in meetings where up to 50% of that time is wasted

- up to 90% of mergers and acquisitions that look great on paper fail to deliver the promised value, in part because employees aren't engaged and relationships aren't managed

Just for a moment, imagine yourself at work and in a meeting – a type of interaction that's an all too common occurrence in today's business world. As you sit there, perhaps you find yourself thinking…

"I wish she'd stop talking."

"He's repeating himself, again."

"How is this relevant?"

"If only I could just get a word in edgeways."

CHAPTER 1

"I want to say something but I don't want to embarrass myself."

"Even when I make suggestions I feel like nobody's listening to me."

"Can't you just get to the point?"

Fig 1. Inner Thoughts

If even a few of these reactions have passed through your mind during meetings, then this book will come to your aid. It seeks to provide you with practical strategies to get your views across and to manage situations and interactions in constructive and skilful ways. You'll learn how to use the behaviours that foster success in your collaborative endeavours, helping you to achieve positive task outcomes and build great relationships.

It's useful to begin by thinking about your own situation at work and how you interact with others. Perhaps you're one of the quieter folk around – someone who likes to think before speaking, gather information before reaching a decision, plan before acting, and persevere with a task. If so, then you're in the company of the roughly 38% of the workforce popularly branded as 'Introverts'. Despite the fact that the business world is dominated by 'Extroverts', introverts of all cultures can learn new behavioural strategies that will help them reclaim some of the territory whilst retaining their identity.

On the other hand, you may be one of the more talkative people in interactions: someone who is stimulated by talking with others, happy to ad lib, and with a preference for thinking things out by talking them through. If so, then you are more likely to be an extrovert. And if the cap fits, you too can learn behavioural strategies that will help you to increase your effectiveness at work.

Of course, things are rarely this simple. As Carl Jung, the founder of analytical psychology, once said: "There is no such thing as a pure introvert or extrovert. Such a person would be in the lunatic asylum." The reality is that each of us is a mixture.

In this book I argue that, irrespective of your own personal style, Behaviour Analysis is the key to your behavioural success. Behaviour Analysis is a remarkable tool with a long history and many associated success stories. It was pioneered in the late 1960s by research psychologists Neil Rackham, Peter Honey and Terry Morgan. In their research they observed people in a variety of work settings to determine the answer to the question: "What is it that differentiates the most successful teams and individuals from the average?" They wanted to tease out the "success" behaviours so that more people could benefit from understanding these behaviours and develop more effective ways of interacting.

I first learned about their work in 1989 when I trained in Behaviour Analysis at Huthwaite Research Group. As I worked with clients in financial and professional services, I was quickly aware of the impact Behaviour Analysis had on the people it touched. Since then I've used Behaviour Analysis when working with thousands of clients drawn from thirty or so different nationalities and spread across three continents. Building on the pioneers' work, together with my colleagues I have been able to unearth new findings and share new discoveries about how this simple but incredibly powerful tool can be used.

Every time I use Behaviour Analysis I see the proverbial light-bulb come on; I witness the 'aha' moment when clients experience an insight that causes them to see their world and how they behave in it very differently. One of my clients, an auditor, describes Behaviour Analysis as "the most powerful tool I have come across". That's quite a testimonial, coming as it does from a highly educated person whose job is to examine and verify information.

An introduction to Behaviour Analysis

One reason people like Behaviour Analysis is because it's an objective measure of an interaction. Quite simply, it's a way to record verbal behaviour, capturing everything that's said in any interaction in real time and using that data as feedback to develop future behaviour.

Behaviour Analysis enables trained behavioural observers to record what was *actually* said (rather than what you thought you had said or would have liked to say). This objectivity brings a rigour that instils confidence in even the most sceptical of people. This book reveals the background to that rigour and will help you to understand how Behaviour Analysis has traditionally been used. More than that, it offers you a do-it-yourself guide to Behaviour Analysis with a view to helping you manage your own behavioural development. Aided by clear explanations and practical examples, you will acquire the tools to build new behavioural muscle, create better behavioural habits, increase your behavioural repertoire and have greater impact on all those with whom you work.

Why behaviour?

What you say and what you do constitutes your behaviour and it is deeply influenced by your experience, background and culture. Deborah Tannen's work on the influence of linguistic style reveals that ways of speaking learned in childhood affect how you are judged and how you are listened to. Moreover, the linguistic style of women is different from what is natural to men. There is much that both sexes can learn from each other.

Most of the time you have control over your behaviour and can exercise choice about how you behave. Personality, on the other hand, denotes who you are and is much less open to change. Your behaviours influence the impact you have. It's how you negotiate relationships, and demonstrates how you can make a difference. Furthermore, behaviour breeds behaviour, and so the way you behave shapes the responses you get from others.

Building behavioural flexibility early in your career helps you set yourself apart from the crowd and become a role model for your peers. Your emotional intelligence develops through understanding the impact your behaviour has on others, and vice versa. As you transition from an individual contributor role to being a supervisor and then a manager, so your behavioural repertoire needs to extend. The more senior you are in an organisation, the greater your need for behavioural flexibility and the ability to shift your focus to myriad tasks: strategic direction, leadership, influencing, decision-making, building commitment to change.

When you ask people to describe the leaders who have inspired them they use phrases such as: "good listener", "always seems interested", "focussed", "supportive". These descriptors are *behaviours* and Behaviour Analysis makes them tangible.

So how does Behaviour Analysis work in practice?

Think of almost any interaction in business and there's scope to use Behaviour Analysis. It's very easy. Traditionally, a trained behavioural analyst observes a group of people: a management team, perhaps, or a cross-functional project group. The observer does precisely that: she observes you, capturing your interactions in a series of behavioural categories.

Behaviour categories

A behaviour category is a way of describing a behaviour and of distinguishing between behaviours. Simple examples are:

Seeking Information (the category used when a question is asked), for example:

"How many people are coming to the meeting?"

"Why do you think we need to change the performance appraisal system?"

and

Giving Information (the category used to capture opinions, reasons, and facts that have been expressed), for example:

"Six people are expected to come to the meeting."

"I think there's mounting evidence to suggest that the traditional approach to performance management doesn't achieve the intended outcome."

Fig 2. Seeking Information and Giving Information

By using these descriptive categories, Behaviour Analysis provides a language for interactions that can be used regardless of an individual's education, profession or work setting.

Neil Rackham and Peter Honey started using Behaviour Analysis with a basic 11-category model. I have extended this over the years to a 15-category model, based on my observations of additional behaviours that have a positive impact in a wide range of business interactions; for example: group work, project team meetings, performance conversations. I have used these 15 categories with teams in industries as diverse as financial services, food manufacturing, petrochemicals, utilities, government and professional services. And our work has embraced many different cultures and nationalities, from China to Canada and from Sweden to South Africa.

Any behavioural categories selected for observation have to meet five criteria. This ensures that any two trained observers will be consistent in their observations. Meeting the criteria also increases the reliability of the data, providing an accurate picture of what was said. The five criteria are:

- **Measurable** – It's important that the category can be measured accurately. Something that you say is much easier to measure accurately than your non-verbal behaviour. Verbal behaviour is broadly sequential (one contribution after another) whereas non-verbal behaviour is simultaneous (everyone in the group is behaving non-verbally all the time).

- **Distinct** – Each category must be distinct from another. The MECE framework developed in McKinsey & Company by Barbara Minto asserts that any categorisation should be *mutually exclusive* and *collectively exhaustive*. In other words, each category must be clearly defined, with no overlap or ambiguity. For example, 'Asking questions' is distinct from 'Summarising'. In addition, *'collectively exhaustive'* means that the categories used should take into account all the possible options.

- **Meaningful** – The category must make sense to the world in which the people in the interaction are operating (representational validity). Behaviours relating to successful teams are used with teams and groups. Different success behaviours would be used with salespeople or negotiators.

- **Open to change** – Unlike personality, behaviours can be and are changed. Behaviour Analysis focuses on the changes you *can* make. It's not always easy but it is eminently possible.

- **Related to success** – The work of the Behavioural Analysis pioneers (Rackham, Honey, Evison, Morgan, Colbert) sought to highlight what differentiated successful performers from average or unsuccessful ones. On this basis they identified 'success models' for a range of interactions. I have retained that focus in my own work. After all, why would you want to train or coach people to use behaviours that were anything other than successful?

With an appreciation of what Behaviour Analysis is and how we select categories for observing a team, let's now look at the 15 categories. For ease of reference, each of the behaviour categories is grouped into one of five clusters of behaviour developed from Rackham's original work on behavioural classification:

Initiating behaviours	how ideas are managed in interactions
Reacting behaviours	how other people's contributions are evaluated
Expressing behaviours	how an individual's personal emotional state is revealed
Clarifying behaviours	how information, opinion, facts and reasons are expressed
Process behaviours	how the airtime is shared in the interaction

CHAPTER 1

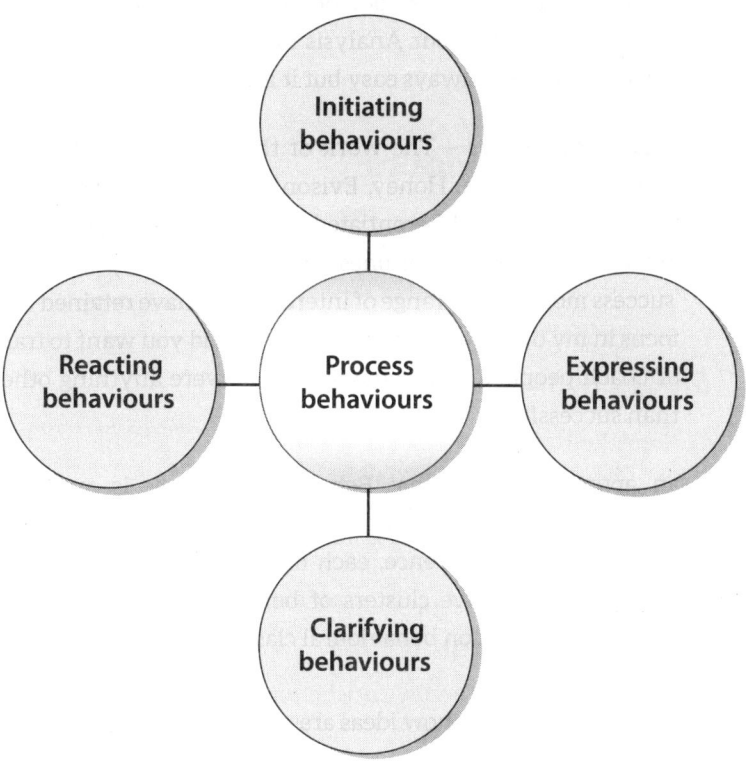

Fig 3. Five Clusters of Behaviour

All five clusters are present in successful interactions, although the proportions vary.

We will now explore each cluster in turn, identifying the name of each category within it, providing a definition of the category, and including an example. (Further examples of each category can be found in Appendix A.)

Behaviour Analysis Fifteen Category Model

Initiating behaviours:

There are four categories in this cluster: Proposing Procedure, Proposing Content, Building, and Seeking Proposals.

1. Proposing Procedure

This category involves the suggesting of a new course of action. It relates to the way in which a pair or group is working – or could work. For example: *"Shall we start by discussing the graduate scheme, then we can come onto the HR plan for the year?"*

2. Proposing Content

This involves suggesting a new concept or idea which is actionable and which relates to the topic being discussed: *"Let's create some opportunities for our graduates to work-shadow."*

3. Building

This category covers efforts to extend or develop a proposal already made by another person: *"Yes, and we could have them rotate through the different departments."*

4. Seeking Proposals

This relates to directly asking another, or others, for a proposal or build (see 1-3 above): *"What would you suggest we do with them?"*

Reacting behaviours:
Supporting, Disagreeing and Defending–Attacking

5. Supporting

Making a clear statement of agreement with, or support for, a person or their statement, opinion, idea or approach; for example: *"That's a great suggestion."*

6. Disagreeing

Making a clear statement of disagreement with someone else's statement, opinion, idea or approach, or raising objections to such a contribution, as in: *"I don't think that will work."*

7. Defending–Attacking

Attacking another person (as distinct from an issue) directly, or defending yourself against an attack. Such behaviour is usually judgmental and emotional; for example: *"That sounds like just another way to get someone to do your donkey work, lazy-bones."*

Expressing behaviours:
Giving Feelings and Open

8. Giving Feelings

An expression of your feelings about the current situation or work in progress, as in: *"I'm uncomfortable that we haven't explored all the possibilities."*

9. Open

Non-defensive admissions of mistakes or inadequacies; for example: *"I'm sorry, maybe I haven't thought it through well enough."*

Clarifying behaviours:

Giving Information, Seeking Information, Testing Understanding and Summarising

10. Giving Information

Making a statement of fact, or giving an opinion or reason to another person(s): *"We have five graduates joining IT this year."*

11. Seeking Information

Seeking facts, opinions or reasons from other(s): *"Are all five joining at the same time?"*

12. Testing Understanding

Checking out an assumption or checking whether a previous contribution has been correctly understood: *"Did you say five?"*

13. Summarising

Repeating accurately and in a condensed form (with nothing new) the content of all or part of the preceding discussion: *"We are discussing the graduate scheme. We've had an idea about rotating the graduates through the departments that has had a mixed reception and we know that we have five graduates joining IT."*

Process behaviours:

Shutting Out and Bringing In. These two process behaviours can only be used in tandem with one of the thirteen mentioned above.

14. Shutting Out

Behaving in a way that prevents or shortens another's contribution – most typically, cutting across a speaker by interrupting and/or answering a question posed to someone else:

"….can I just make a point…?"

15. Bringing In

Seeking a contribution from a person who has not contributed for some time or at all; for example: *"Ian, what do you think?"*

The fifteen categories: judgment-free

It should be emphasised that none of the 15 categories listed above judges the value of a contribution. None of these behaviours is either 'good' or 'bad'; rather, the categories simply attempt to capture what took place. Decisions about the appropriateness of any particular behaviour, or sequence of behaviours, rest with those who participated in the interaction. The nature of the interaction itself is also relevant. For example, in a brainstorming session you would expect to see lots of Proposing Content and no Disagreeing, whereas in a performance review there is likely to be a higher incidence of Proposing Procedure and Seeking Information.

Behaviour budget

All of us have what I call a 'behaviour budget': the quantum of behaviours we 'spend' in our interactions. We're unlikely to be mindful about how we're going to spend that budget, and this can lead us to be profligate, to spend our budget on unsuitable behaviours, or even to underspend. However, once we're aware of which behaviours to use, we can make conscious choices about *how* to spend our behaviour budget. By this means we can turn up the dial on our effectiveness, selecting behaviours that have a positive influence on outcomes, process and relationships. As the actress Stella Adler once said: "In your choices lies your talent."

Where other topics have entered the development arena with a splash, only to be over-taken by the next innovation, Behaviour Analysis has consistently been adding value without fanfare or notoriety for almost 50 years. As businesses make increasing demands on people to do more, do better and do faster, and as people are exhorted to cross both functions and geographical boundaries (both in person and via technology), the currency of behavioural skills rises ever higher.

It's time for Behaviour Analysis to come of age.

Summary of key points

- Behaviour Analysis is a research-based tool geared to improving personal and team effectiveness

- There are five clusters of behaviour: Initiating, Reacting, Expressing, Clarifying and Process

- The five clusters break down into a 15-category model for analysing group interactions and feeding back results to raise awareness, build insight and drive action towards the goal of positive behavioural change

- No behaviour category is either 'good' or 'bad'; it is about what is appropriate in a given context

- Behaviour Analysis will support you in remedying unhelpful behavioural habits

- You have a behavioural budget. How you spend that budget is influenced by your awareness and skill

How to use this book

There are various ways in which you can use this book. You can read it cover-to-cover and then return to the sections that seem most useful for you. Alternatively, you can begin by selecting the chapters that appeal to you most (refer to the Contents page and/or the chapter overviews below) and dip in and out of the book. Each chapter has a summary of its key points for the time-poor reader. And for those of you who prefer to dwell on a topic and deepen your learning, there is a selection of exercises for you to complete. Finally, at the back of the book there are some suggestions for how you can start to experiment with applying Behaviour Analysis at work.

The following chapters

The following chapters address how Behaviour Analysis is used together with specific behaviours from the 15-category model. By studying these you can deepen your understanding of each category and how you can use it – effectively. You can then decide which categories of behavioural muscle you would like to build.

Chapter 2 provides you with an overview of how we use Behaviour Analysis to help people to develop greater behavioural effectiveness. It also offers examples of behavioural data.

Chapter 3 focuses on the subject of managing meetings and explores how you can save both time and money whilst enhancing your behavioural skills.

In Chapter 4 we explore the behaviours that help you to establish your presence in interactions and manage the level of your contributions.

With ideas being a critical element in the continuing prosperity of a business, Chapter 5 explores how ideas are both generated and managed.

How you respond to ideas and people and how you constructively reveal your emotions form the focus of Chapters 6 and 7.

In Chapter 8 you'll learn about the two key influencing styles and how best to leverage these in your daily work.

To address the increasingly familiar topic of remote interactions and virtual teamwork, Chapter 9 focuses on behaviours that help conference calls be more effective.

Finally, Chapter 10 helps you to consider how you can secure a return on investment from learning about and using Behaviour Analysis.

At the end of the book you will find references to academic sources. In addition, there are three appendices with material to support you as you use Behaviour Analysis at work.

CHAPTER 2
Using Behaviour Analysis

"Whatever words we utter should be chosen with care, for people will hear them and be influenced by them for good or ill."

Gautama Siddhartha (the Buddha)

How is Behaviour Analysis used?

Conventional Behaviour Analysis uses an experienced observer working with individuals and teams. Understanding how this works will help you to see how Behaviour Analysis facilitates skill development. Later on you'll find out how to use elements of Behaviour Analysis independent of a skilled observer.

Using Behaviour Analysis with an observer follows a process of:

Observation

Feedback

Action

Impact

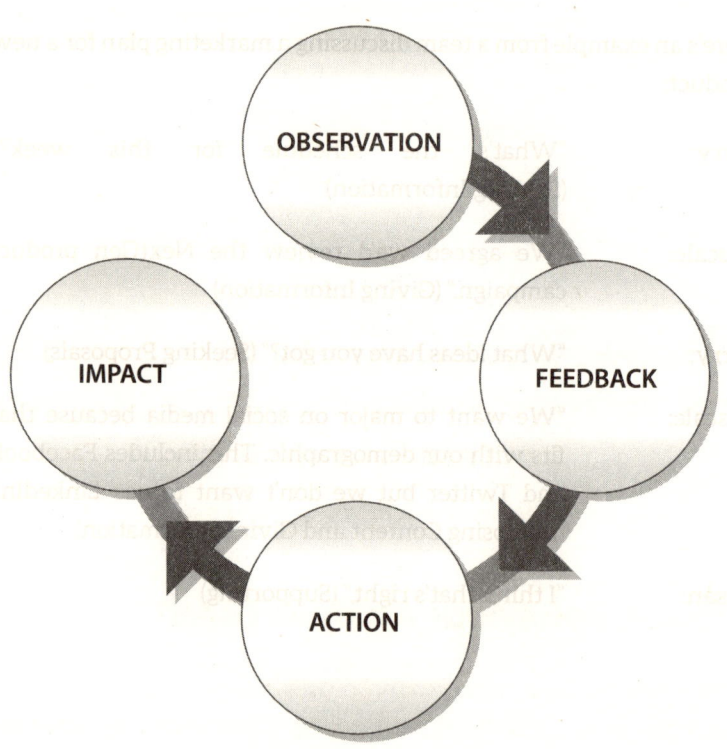

Fig 4. Behaviour Analysis Process

Observation

Working closely with a group of people, the behaviour analyst observes their interactions. Every time a member of the group says something the analyst captures that contribution in one of the categories, or a combination of them. As it takes considerable skill to listen to all the contributions from group members and capture them accurately, observers are highly trained and frequently test the accuracy of their work.

Here's an example from a team discussing a marketing plan for a new product:

Jerry:	"What's the schedule for this week?" (Seeking Information)
Pascale:	"We agreed we'd review the NextGen product campaign." (Giving Information)
Jerry:	"What ideas have you got?" (Seeking Proposals)
Pascale:	"We want to major on social media because that fits with our demographic. This includes Facebook and Twitter but we don't want to use LinkedIn." (Proposing Content and Giving Information)
Susan:	"I think that's right." (Supporting)

TIME	Start:	Finish:	Duration:
GROUP	Marketing		

BEHAVIOUR	PERSON		
	JERRY	PASCALE	SUSAN
Proposing Procedure			
Proposing Content		I	
Building			
Seeking Proposals	I		
Supporting			I
Disagreeing			
Defending/Attacking			
Open			
Giving Feelings			
Giving Information		II	
Seeking Information	I		
Testing Understanding			
Summarising			
TOTAL			
Shutting Out			
Bringing In			

Fig 5. Behaviour Observation Form - 1

Each behaviour contribution is marked in the appropriate category box.

Opposite you can see the data from observing a project team in a 20-minute session on milestone planning:

CHAPTER 2

TIME	Start: 10:00am Finish: 10:20am Duration: 20 mins				
GROUP	Marketing - Milestone Planning				
	PERSON			
BEHAVIOUR	ROMAN	KATE	BRUNO	OLIVER
Proposing Procedure	㇐㇐㇐ IIII		III	
Proposing Content	㇐㇐ ㇐㇐ IIII	IIII	㇐㇐	㇐㇐ I
Building		IIII	II	III
Seeking Proposals	I	IIII		
Supporting	III	III	II	I
Disagreeing	㇐㇐ III		II	I
Defending/Attacking				
Open				
Giving Feelings				
Giving Information	㇐㇐ ㇐㇐ ㇐㇐ ㇐㇐ ㇐㇐ ㇐㇐ ㇐㇐ IIII	㇐㇐ ㇐㇐ ㇐㇐ IIII	㇐㇐ ㇐㇐ ㇐㇐ ㇐㇐ II	㇐㇐ ㇐㇐ ㇐㇐ II
Seeking Information	II	㇐㇐ III	㇐㇐ III	
Testing Understanding	IIII	III	I	
Summarising	II		II	
TOTAL	82	45	47	28
Shutting Out	II	III	III	IIII
Bringing In		II		

Fig 6. Behaviour Observation Form – 2

The table is organised by columns, one per team member. Each mark in each category represents a contribution made by the person whose name is at the top of that column. In this example you can, for example, see that Roman used Summarising behaviour twice and that Bruno made 22 contributions that were Giving Information.

This data tells us what each person and the team did – in other words, how they spent their behavioural budget. It also shows where there are gaps in the team's behaviour. It does not tell us whether, for example, Oliver was feeling bored or if Kate wanted to say more.

Feedback

Over time the behaviour analyst captures enough data to share with the group. We call this a data 'snapshot' because it's a picture of what happened at a given point in time. It captures, accurately, the behaviours the team members used. By exploring the data, group members can very quickly gain insights into how they – and others – typically behave, how effective they are and what behavioural alternatives might be open to them.

The observer can share the data in a variety of ways. The choice about how best to help group members understand the data is driven by what has been observed, with the aim of making the data relevant, meaningful and powerful.

If we take the project team example (above), we can ask questions like:

- How has the airtime been shared?
- How did you handle Kate's (low-level) participation?
- How well was the meeting managed?
- How well did you explore each other's ideas?
- What was the impact of the high levels of Shutting Out?

The quantitative Behaviour Analysis data will often be accompanied by qualitative observations from the group, creating a rich picture, deepening understanding and increasing insight. Ways of collecting qualitative data include:

- Inviting the team to rate their satisfaction with the *process* (how they worked together) and the *outcome* (how successful) on a scale of 1 to 5, where 1 = low satisfaction and 5 = high satisfaction

- Eliciting adjectives to describe the meeting: for example, productive, frustrating, energetic, confusing

- Asking for adjectives to describe each of the participants: for example, helpful, supportive, dominating, quiet

Drawing together the qualitative and quantitative data, the observer can help you to reflect on your personal data by asking questions like:

- How typical is this of how you behave at work?

- What do you recognise?

- What has surprised you?

- What effect did your behaviours have?

- Where are you behaviourally strong?

- Where are there opportunities for development and why might this be important/valuable?

It's important that you make sense of your data in a way that maximises its helpfulness to you and the contexts in which you work.

Action

By exploring the data and the different categories, you can identify – individually and collectively – the behavioural changes you need to make to improve your performance. Since all of us are a 'work in progress', there's always an opportunity to do better, be more effective, have more impact. The real skill is in selecting the one or two behaviours that, if developed further, will have a significant impact on our performance. And it's almost always easier to do *more* of a particular behaviour than less.

Impact

The purpose of making any behavioural change is to be more effective. Therefore it's important that you measure the impact. Did the change in behaviour have the desired effect?

Here's what a manufacturing manager had to say about Behaviour Analysis:

> *It has been really helpful for me to learn about Behaviour Analysis. I hadn't appreciated the impact I was having on the team. Since the feedback I have made regular attempts to lead the meetings in a more structured and efficient way. The feedback has been very positive and we have reduced the time spent in meetings.*

The process of Observation-Feedback-Action-Impact also helps you remedy communication problems and break unhelpful behavioural patterns. Here's an example of an unhelpful behavioural pattern, one which restricted the participation of others during meetings:

> *George was the leader of a senior management team in a multinational petrochemical business. Deeply committed to the idea of engaging his people in team discussions, he regularly asked questions to elicit their thoughts, opinions and ideas. However, each time George asked a question he immediately followed it with his own answer. This was unhelpful because it blocked the opportunity for his team to contribute. Worse than that, because he had already shared his viewpoint or ideas, it was unlikely that the team members were going to disagree with their boss. The team lost the chance to explore options.*

When the data gathered by the observer was shared with George he was surprised. He was not aware of his behavioural habit, or the consequences for the team. Now alert to the downsides of his behaviour he was able to determine what he needed to do differently.

Sometimes people ask me: "Now you've told us all about the behaviours and what constitutes success, isn't there a risk that we will adapt our behaviour just to be seen to be doing the right thing?" Now, that's a challenge I welcome, and here's why: you can only learn to do things differently when you're conscious of the change you are trying to make.

Four Stages for Learning New Skills

Burch's 'Four Stages For Learning New Skills' identifies the phases you go through when improving a skill or behaviour.

```
LEVEL 4
Unconsciously Skilled

LEVEL 3
Consciously Skilled

LEVEL 2
Consciously Unskilled

LEVEL 1
Unconsciously Unskilled
```

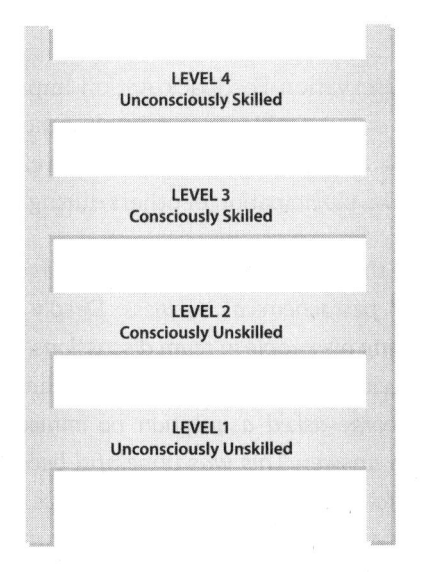

Developed by former GTI employee, Noel Burch in 1977.
Reproduced with kind permission of Gordon Training International

Fig 7. Four Stages For Learning New Skills

In the first phase – **Unconsciously Unskilled** – you're unaware of the level and range of your behavioural skill. This lack of understanding can lead you to carry on blithely, ignorant of the impact of your behaviour and the potential opportunities for improvement.

In the second phase – **Consciously Unskilled** – the blinkers have been lifted. You're now aware of your behaviours and their impact on others. The 'Feedback' phase of the Behaviour Analysis cycle (Observation, Feedback, Action, Impact) is the mechanism by which you gain that awareness and is a critical stage of your self-development.

The third phase – **Consciously Skilled** – is where you take 'Action'. This is the opportunity to experiment with new behaviours, to play with the specific categories and to build new behavioural muscle. As with learning any new skill it can feel a little clunky to begin with. It's helpful here to reflect on your experience of, say, learning a musical instrument or taking up a new sport. How many times did you make mistakes? How often did you have to practise to see an improvement? How long did it take you to reach an acceptable standard? Or consider a situation where you've been asked to adopt a new way of working: for example, a behaviour-based safety system or continuous improvement practices. It's likely you won't succeed on all fronts from the outset but with practice you'll build both competence and confidence.

As you try to do things differently, it's realistic to expect that this won't be easy. Nothing worth having ever is. It's important to persist in your practice and resist the temptation to abandon ship when things feel a little uncomfortable. Discomfort is a good sign. Neurologically, discomfort arises when our brain is trying to make sense of something new. So hang on in there as your brain adapts, builds new neural pathways and opens up more resources for you to leverage. As the saying goes: "Practice makes perfect."

The fourth and final phase of learning – **Unconsciously Skilled** – occurs when you have practised to the extent that your brain uses heuristics, accessing the skilled behaviour at the right time in the right place with effortless ease.

I've witnessed some remarkable and skilful transformations in teams where Behaviour Analysis has been adopted, helping people shift from unconsciously unskilled to consciously skilled. (Unconsciously skilled tends to follow later, as a result of further purposeful practice.)

> On one occasion, the head of a technology leadership team approached me, unhappy that his leaders weren't communicating well with each other. They adopted functional 'expert' positions, creating silos and barriers to collaboration. Meetings were characterised by arguments and competition for airtime. Using Behaviour Analysis we observed the team over the course of the afternoon. Having captured reliable and sufficient data we explained to the team what we'd been doing and gave a presentation on the basics of Behaviour Analysis. Having established a shared level of understanding, we then revealed their data, highlighting some important points that revealed critical information about how the team was (or was not) working.
>
> We worked with the team, helping them interrogate the data and understand the impact of their behaviour. When we contrasted their data with that from high performing teams, the gap was enough to motivate them to take action. We were able to help them to identify both a collective goal and individual behavioural goals. Everyone knew what every other member of the team was setting out to achieve and made a commitment to support one another in making these changes.
>
> Two months later we returned to observe another meeting with the same team. The picture the data created couldn't have been more different. They had honoured their commitment to behave

differently and had done a great job of supporting each other. In subsequent months, as these leaders worked with their own teams, they shared their understanding of Behaviour Analysis to help drive similar levels of improvement.

When I asked the leadership team what had accounted for their success they replied:

"Behaviour Analysis is really useful because it's objective. It was humbling to see just how badly we were behaving. It's helped us to avoid futile 'tit for tat' discussions and concentrate on more respectful and constructive dialogue." One leader commented: "I now enjoy coming to our meetings – I never thought I'd hear myself say that!"

By using the Behaviour Analysis process of Observe, Feedback, Action, Impact, you develop an understanding of the behaviours related to effective performance and an appreciation of your own behavioural skills profile. The insights gained thereby help you determine what behaviours you will develop to enhance your performance, allowing you to grow in skills and confidence as you thrive on the oxygen of new experience.

Summary of key points

- Using Behaviour Analysis follows a four-step process of Observation, Feedback, Action and Impact

- Building new behavioural habits will increase your flexibility, helping you operate in a skilful and distinctive way

- Building behavioural skill follows Burch's Four Stages For Learning

- Working with Behaviour Analysis has produced significant results across a range of industries and cultures

- The combination of quantitative data and qualitative discussion provides rich learning based on objective observations and personal perspectives

CHAPTER 3

Making Meetings Effective

> "Meetings are indispensible when you don't want to do anything."
>
> John Kenneth Galbraith

Meetings are a regular feature of business interactions and we bemoan their inefficiencies. Can I invite you to reflect on how much of your time is spent in meetings? Take a look at the following questions and answer them Yes/No, based on your experience:

1. I spend too much time in meetings

2. Many meetings I attend lack focus

3. Meetings are frequently dominated by one or two people

4. There's little opportunity to discuss things in the meetings I attend

5. People frequently talk over each other in meetings

6. We work through the agenda

7. We run out of time

8. We agree the outcome we're hoping to achieve ahead of each item

9. The meetings are slow and boring

10. The meetings can be chaotic

Now score your responses:

Questions 1, 2, 3, 4, 5, 7, 9, 10   1 point for each question with the answer 'Yes'

Questions 6, 8   1 point for each question with the answer 'No'

A score of 5 or more points is dangerous but familiar territory. It reflects the parlous state of our meetings culture. In every organisation I've worked with, regardless of industry or geography, there's a constant lament about the number of hours spent in meetings and the waste of time involved. People complain that they can't get anything done because they're always in meetings. And yet meetings are essential. So how can you extend your behavioural skills to ensure that the time you spend in meetings is both effective and efficient? What could you do with the additional time if you were to improve the performance of your meetings by just 10%?

Chapter 3

Four Strategies

I'm frequently invited to observe teams in meetings. Whether the meeting involves a project team, a board, a cross-functional team, or a sales team, more often than not it falls short in some way. Over the years my colleagues and I have been able to identify some of the traps meetings are vulnerable to. On this basis, we've been able to identify **four strategies** to avoid the typical pitfalls, strategies which successful teams use to good effect.

Thankfully, these strategies are easy to learn and, with practice, become increasingly easy to apply. What's more, employing these strategies helps make those attending meetings more engaged, energised, committed and inclined to give of their time. And who would argue against that?

The four strategies are:

1. *Balance task and process*

2. *Provide clear structure*

3. *Ensure clarity*

4. *Encourage participation*

Whilst they sound deceptively simple, you'll doubtless know, from painful experience, that most meetings fail to deploy at least one of these strategies, if not all four.

In the rest of this chapter we'll explore each strategy in turn to identify how meetings can be kept on track.

1. Balance task and process

Nowadays there's a recurring mantra I hear in many of my clients' businesses: "Do more with less." This is symptomatic of organisations facing cutbacks or under mounting competitive threat; the pressure is on to drive down costs.

Pressure to 'just get it done' means that more and more people focus exclusively on the task. They operate under beliefs like: "As long as we complete the task everything will be OK", "We need to get this done regardless of what it costs", or "I'm measured on outputs so that's where I'll concentrate my time."

The fallacy here is that the task is the only aspect of work that matters. If the task is all, who cares if you alienate people along the way? What does it matter if you railroad your stakeholders? Why bother to consult others for ideas when you can do this yourself? In this type of climate, technical experts will immerse themselves in the details of the task, neglectful of other responsibilities and reinforcing the view that they are "nerds", "geeks" and "automatons" with "no people skills". Overly confident people will push on regardless, convinced by the strength of their own ideas.

No matter how important the task is, there's a second dimension that needs your attention when managing meetings, and that is the **process**: the way in which we work together to achieve the task; how we organise the time and ourselves.

Meetings that score highly in terms of effectiveness are those that address both the Task and the Process. The meeting balances the demands of both. The precise balance is influenced by the time that's available, the resourcefulness of those at the meeting, and what's appropriate for the task or topic under discussion.

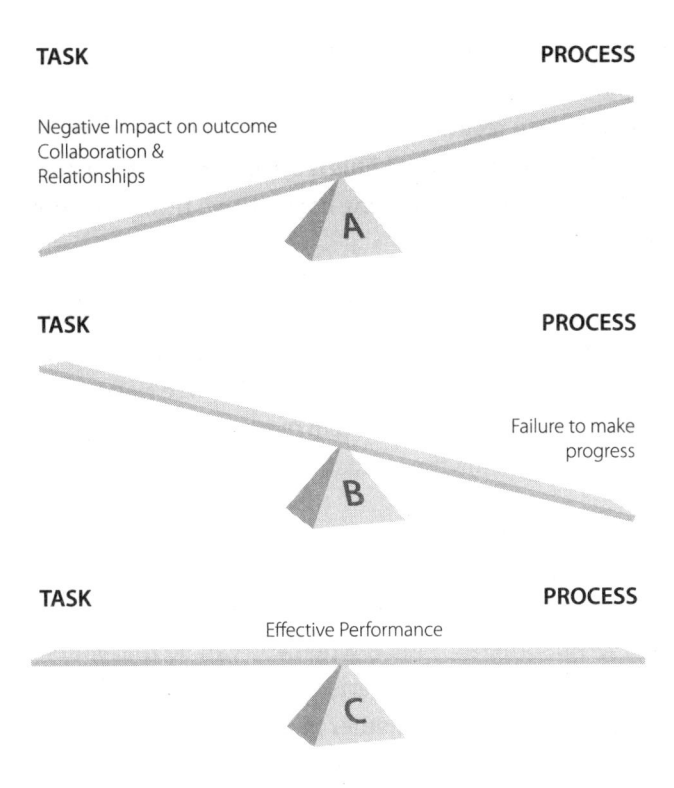

Fig 8. Three Dimensions of Task and Process

Figure 8 (above) illustrates that Task at the expense of Process (a) is expensive in terms of effectiveness, morale and relationships. Process at the expense of Task (b) is usually a recipe for failing to get anything completed. Equilibrium between the two dimensions (c) is where your focus needs to be. In this way you achieve the task in the most resource-effective and relationship-positive way.

This balance is best achieved by having a member of the meeting who is dedicated to managing the process rather than the task: in most cases, a chairperson or a meetings manager. Ideally this individual would not have a vested interest in the outcome of the meeting, or section of the meeting.

Studies on leadership have revealed very different styles. In one such study by Boyatzis, Rochford and Jack, 'Task Oriented Leadership' is contrasted with 'Socio-emotional Leadership'. Task oriented leadership focuses on getting the job done, whereas the socio-emotional leader deals with relational matters. What we learn from the research is that effective leadership requires both styles. However, since the two styles require very different neural networks to be operating, your brain cannot run both networks simultaneously. People who manage both networks create time for them separately and/or put more than one type of leader in place so that both are attended to. And it's the same in meetings. The Chair cannot run both networks successfully.

As an effective Chair, instead of trying to address your views on the task *and* manage the requirements of the process, you can concentrate on the process alone and help the rest of the group manage their relationship to the task. This is best achieved through the skilful use of questioning to help those in the meeting explore and better understand what is being discussed. As Chair, you facilitate others' understanding rather than focus on ensuring they understand your views.

"That's nice in theory, but..." I hear you saying. Indeed, achieving this is often quite a challenge if you're the 'Chair' *and* you have a point of view on what's under discussion. So what can you do about this? Fortunately you have a number of options:

- Share your perspective with people before the meeting – help people understand your thinking without trying to manipulate their thinking (Giving Information).

- Take a step back and reflect on questions such as: "Is my perspective really value-adding?" or "Is it only me who can get to the right solution here?" or "How can I help the group to extend their thinking to include some of the things I've been considering?"

- Be open with the team about the tension you're experiencing and ask for their help (Giving Feelings and Seeking Proposals).

- Ask another member of the meeting to chair the items that beg for your contribution (Procedural Proposal). This can also be used as a development opportunity for team members: with luck, they'll soon be referring to you as a role model for effective meetings management.

- Wait until the end of the discussion and then share your perspective (Giving Information). However, there may be a need to add further time for discussion if you employ this strategy, since others may want to respond to your input.

- Use coloured 'hats' (Edward de Bono's 'Thinking Hats'), either literally or figuratively. For example, when you don the 'blue' hat you're in Chair mode, while putting on the 'white' hat signals that you're contributing facts.

If you're the Chair or the meetings manager, you need above all to resist the temptation to get stuck into the content whilst at the same time managing the process. Disclosing your bias on the task risks closing down potential contributions from the rest of the team. This can often be the case where you're the boss in a hierarchical environment or where people might not trust your motives. It can be hard for the meeting members to share an opposing view if the conditions for openness have not been established.

> Marina was the Head of Global R&D for a manufacturing business. She got some 360° feedback where the message was: "You need to delegate more" and "Be less controlling in meetings". When this was explored with her, Marina explained that because of her deep expertise she found it hard to trust her staff to come up with the right solutions. This was particularly evident in meetings, where she would raise a client issue and then tell people what she wanted them to do. Her aim was to help her staff but her behaviour had

the opposite effect. The team – and particularly those who worked most closely with the client – started to feel disempowered and over time their contributions in meetings got fewer and fewer until it almost became the Marina one-woman show. Morale in the team suffered and people started to avoid meetings.

Marina began to realise the impact her behaviour was having. Instead of putting her energy into getting her ideas across she focussed on identifying the areas where she could risk relinquishing some of her control over the content and use her expertise to help her team to develop their ideas. She achieved this through skilful questioning and demonstrating her ability to listen (Seeking Proposals, Seeking Information, Testing Understanding and Summarising), thereby empowering and guiding the team.

Measuring your progress

In the effort to balance task with process, it's useful for the Chair not simply to measure their own personal progress but also engage the team in monitoring progress within the meeting as a whole. The best examples of a progress review come from Ingrid Bens, a leader in the field of facilitation. Ingrid talks about 'Process Check Surveys' and 'Exit Surveys', both of which are simple and straightforward flip-chart exercises that cause a team, group or meeting to consciously reflect on how well they are working together. Here is an example of a Process Check Survey that I frequently use with clients:

CHAPTER 3

HOW ARE WE DOING SO FAR WITH

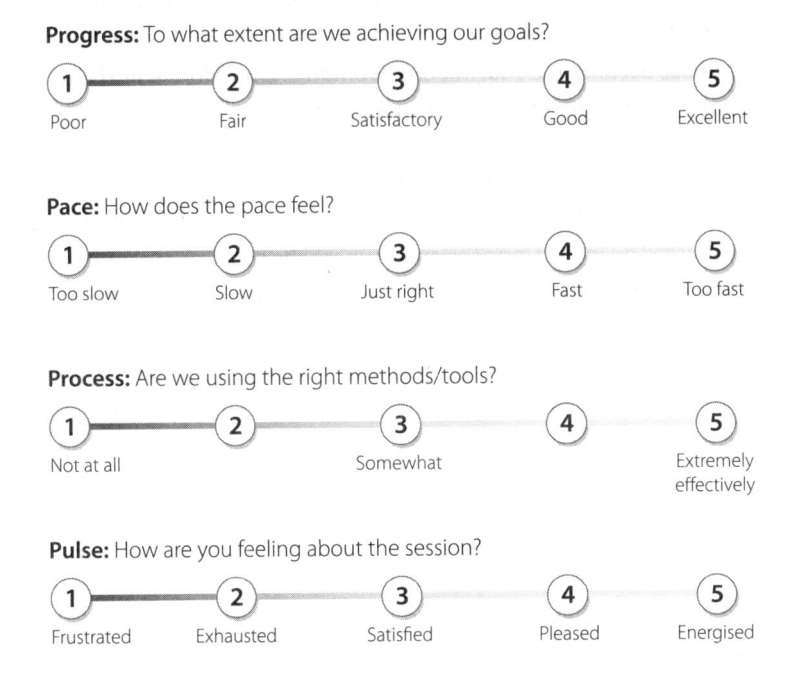

Progress: To what extent are we achieving our goals?

1	2	3	4	5
Poor	Fair	Satisfactory	Good	Excellent

Pace: How does the pace feel?

1	2	3	4	5
Too slow	Slow	Just right	Fast	Too fast

Process: Are we using the right methods/tools?

1	2	3	4	5
Not at all		Somewhat		Extremely effectively

Pulse: How are you feeling about the session?

1	2	3	4	5
Frustrated	Exhausted	Satisfied	Pleased	Energised

Reproduced with kind permission of the author, Ingrid Bens from *Facilitation at a Glance!*

Fig 9. Sample Process Check Survey

It's helpful to use surveys like this both during and at the end of a meeting. For example, during the coffee break you can invite people to place a mark on the survey that reflects their view of how well the team is performing. When you return from the break you can review the scores.

At the end of the meeting you can also use an Exit Survey like the one on the next page:

GIVE YOUR ASSESSMENT OF THE ITEMS BELOW

Output: How well did we achieve what we needed to?

1 — 2 — 3 — 4 — 5
Poor — Fair — Satisfactory — Good — Excellent

Use of Time: How well did we use our time?

1 — 2 — 3 — 4 — 5
Poor — Fair — Satisfactory — Good — Excellent

Participation: How well did we ensure everyone was equally involved?

1 — 2 — 3 — 4 — 5
Poor — Fair — Satisfactory — Good — Excellent

Decision Making: How well thought out were our decisions?

1 — 2 — 3 — 4 — 5
Poor — Fair — Satisfactory — Good — Excellent

Action Plans: How clear and do-able are our action plans?

1 — 2 — 3 — 4 — 5
Poor — Fair — Satisfactory — Good — Excellent

Organisation: How well run was the meeting?

1 — 2 — 3 — 4 — 5
Poor — Fair — Satisfactory — Good — Excellent

Reproduced with kind permission of the author, Ingrid Bens
from *Facilitation at a Glance!*

Fig 10. Sample Exit Survey

A number of organisations use short surveys like this to great effect. But this is not so in every case. For example:

The board of a consultancy, aware of the importance of evaluating the effectiveness of their meetings, acted on this by inviting all attendees to vote a satisfaction score at the end of each meeting. The scoring range was 0-5, where 0=low and 5=excellent. Once the business meeting had finished, the MD (who was also the Chair) asked people for their scores. Everyone contributed a score, along with the rationale for it. And then the meeting was concluded.

The example above reflects positive intent but wasted effort. Concluding the meeting without discussing the results of the survey was a missed opportunity. Whilst it's always useful to have the scores from a survey, the real value lies in the learning that takes place and the action taken to improve the score.

If you take a brief exit survey during the break, before you re-start the agenda you have the opportunity to:

- Look at the scores
- Understand why there are differences
- Identify what's working well
- Ask for suggestions to drive the scores up (or keep them where they need to be)

Then, at the end of the meeting you have the opportunity to collect a second set of scores and inquire:

- What helped?
- What should we keep doing?
- What should we stop doing?
- What should we start doing?

Engaging the team members in the review through your questioning shares the responsibility and encourages all team members to feel they have a part to play in creating an effective process. Having learnt this through your example, team members can then replicate the process review in their own meetings.

2. Provide clear structure

Too many meetings lack clear aims or outcomes; the discussion drifts, often repeating itself. One client has described this feeling of going round in circles as her 'Groundhog Day'. In these meetings that seemingly go nowhere there are frequently side conversations, suggesting people have disconnected from the subject under discussion. And, as the meeting progresses, attendees come and go with no consequence – either literally, because they leave the room, or figuratively, because they're focussed on tablets or phones.

This senselessness arises when there's a lack of agreed structure in the meeting, leading to listlessness and a lack of direction.

The meeting as a journey

The analogy that best describes a meeting with a well-managed structure is that of a journey where everyone knows:

- Where we're heading

- The stops and signposts along the way to help achieve the task

- How long (approximately) it will take

Of course, the route might need to change if you hit a roadblock – but all the same it's useful to have a clear route in mind before starting out.

The more people in the meeting the more structure is needed. Imagine yourself as a tour guide in a busy European city. If you're shepherding a group of 15 tourists you'll need more frequent signposting than when you have just two guests on your tour.

Fig 11. Signposting

The behaviour that helps most in providing structure is Proposing Procedure. Here's a reminder of the definition:

> **Proposing procedure:** Suggesting a new course of action, relating to the way the group is working or could work.

Used effectively, this behaviour occurs throughout the meeting, not just in the opening moments. Here are some examples of how Proposing Procedure can be used at different stages of your meetings:

STAGE	ACTION
At the beginning	*"Let's start by hearing the finance report, followed by sales and then we can focus on HR – recruitment and development - before we finish with AOB."*
During the meeting	*"Pete, can you take notes?"* *"Let's hear from Daniel first and then Petra."* *"Please can we go back to the issue of the recruitment criteria."*
In between topics	*"So that concludes everything on finance, let's now turn our attention to sales. Carol, lead on…"*
Part way through	*"We've covered just one item on the agenda and we're half-way through our time, so I suggest we allocate the remaining time across the outstanding items."* *"Over the break, can I invite you all to place your marks on the exit survey?"* *"Why don't we briefly review the scores on the exit survey and agree any changes we might helpfully make for the remainder of the meeting."*
At the end	*"Thank you for your contributions. I suggest we close the formal proceedings now and spend a little time reviewing how we've done."*

Fig 12. Proposing Procedure at Different Stages of a Meeting

As it's usually the Chair of the meeting who manages the structure, you'd expect this person to score highly on Proposing Procedure. Indeed, in one study by Rackham and Morgan effective Chairs used Proposing Procedure four times more than any other meeting member. Other attendees can also make suggestions about how to organise the time, but in a high-performing team this would not be a high-scoring category for all team members because the Chair would be skilfully managing the process.

Summarising is another behaviour with a particularly positive impact when managing structure in a meeting:

> ***Summarising:*** Repeating, accurately and in a shortened form with no additions, the content of the previous discussion.

Rackham and Morgan's research into the role of the Chairperson revealed that skilled Chairs spent 11.5% of their behavioural budget on Summarising, compared with other members of the meeting who spent, on average, 0.7% of their budget on this behaviour. My own work and that of my colleagues bears out this general finding. Summarising behaviour has the value of:

- Demonstrating that the Chair has accurately listened to the other meeting members
- Helping meeting members arrive at a similar level of understanding
- Demonstrating the Chair's lack of bias

Summarising also provides a platform from which to transition to the next agenda item.

To summarise effectively, a Chair has to stay focused on the subject under discussion and the contributions of the different meeting members rather than his/her opinions.

Sometimes it's not necessary for the Chair's spend on Summarising to be as high as 11.5%. This is when the group has a Scribe to physically capture their notes, actions and decisions somewhere visible to everyone: for example, a flip chart or a white board (see Chapter 4 for more detail on the Scribe). Because people can see the work in progress, this reduces the need for verbal summarising. Nonetheless, Summarising is a behaviour worth practising since it's been shown to be a differentiator in the profile of skilled performers across a range of interactions. In our work, we've observed that the direction of the meeting is clearer when there are at least one or two summaries every 30 minutes.

3. Ensure clarity

When I talk to people about their experience of meetings, an often-expressed frustration is that people seem not to follow up on actions that have been agreed. This disconnect between what happens in the meeting and what subsequently happens outside the meeting accounts for considerable frustration, as well as hours of lost time, involving businesses in needless expense and often negatively impacting working relationships.

When a group of people reconvenes and it becomes clear that actions have not been followed through, it can be embarrassing, humiliating or upsetting. It's not that the 'offenders' deliberately set out to pervert the course of business. More often than not theirs is a sin of omission that they attribute to not understanding what they were supposed to do in the first instance.

> Matteo was a member of a project team. He was new to the team and understandably had been keen to make a good impression. When I first met him he was feeling disengaged from the project manager and unhappy about the progress he was making. As I sought to understand more, Matteo shared that he felt he had let the project manager down because he had failed to follow through on some actions from a meeting that had high visibility in the business. Subsequently the manager had not been delegating work to Matteo. What transpired was that Matteo had not been clear that the actions were his responsibility.

Matteo's situation seems almost unbelievable when viewed in the rational, cold light of day. After all, if everyone pays attention in meetings, surely it follows that all the attendees will be clear about what has been agreed and who is doing what – and by when? In reality, however, attention frequently drifts away in meetings; key points are lost and detail is overlooked.

When working with teams composed of members of different nationalities who are communicating in English (perhaps as a second or third language), we observe that the clarity of what has been agreed is often splintered rather than shared. This is because people are working at different speeds, trying to assimilate information in a language that requires more energy to both understand and express. My colleague Jerry Murphy describes this as the difference between 'breathing' (the involuntary, effortless activity of speaking in your mother tongue) and 'swimming' (the energy-sapping activity of speaking in a non-native language). The meeting often moves on without establishing that shared clarity exists and that people really are on the same page. It's easy to see how any meeting can so readily fall victim to this snare.

Sometimes when working with a group of people over a number of meetings, I'll try a little experiment. Once the meeting has ended I go to each person in turn and ask: "What do you believe has been agreed in the meeting?" I take a note of all the responses and then explore them from two perspectives:

1. To what extent are the responses consistent?

2. How well do the responses match what was actually agreed?

Often there are some surprising findings. In general, however, the responses are more consistent *and* match more closely with what has been agreed when there's someone in the meeting who captures the actions and checks with the group that these actions have been captured correctly (this person may be taking on the role of Minute-taker or Scribe, which is covered in Chapter 4). Also, the level of two specific behaviour categories is higher. The two behaviours that correlate with increased consistency of agreement are: **Testing Understanding** and **Summarising**.

Testing Understanding

Testing Understanding involves a specific type of question which checks that you have understood correctly what someone else has said, or that something you have said has been clearly understood:

- "So do you mean that Peter should lead the team?"

- "Have I been accurate in what I've said?"

Testing Understanding is a helpful way to check your own understanding while ensuring that everyone else in the meeting is following the thread and understanding a specific point in the same way.

Summarising, as you've seen, involves a short, accurate précis of what has been agreed and discussed so far. If you're in a meeting you might summarise for sections of the meeting and/or the entire meeting. By using this behaviour you're recapping what has been said for everyone's benefit, so that everyone *can* be on the same page. Summarising also creates a space where the group can pause and reflect on the progress that's been made thus far. Another quality of an accurate summary is that, used regularly, it controls the pace of the meeting, something that's of particular value where not all members are working in their first language.

Whether you're managing or chairing a meeting, these two behaviours – Testing Understanding and Summarising – are essential to master. They help you ensure that shared clarity exists. If you are not the Chair and these behaviours aren't being used, you have the opportunity to adopt a helpful role. To do this well you have to concentrate on listening to and clarifying the contributions of others. It means being more focused on 'them' rather than on your views, position, or ideas.

> On one occasion I was working with a team of senior consultants in a Big Four firm, exploring the notion of leadership. When I asked the group to identify people they had worked with whom they believed to be good leaders, one of the consultants responded: "I've learned a lot from David. I've noticed that he always takes the time to ensure everyone understands what has been discussed. He does this as much in internal meetings as he does with clients. Just the other week a client remarked to him something along the lines of 'You always demonstrate real care in understanding our discussions'. I thought that was a great remark."

What David had been exercising was his skill in Testing Understanding and Summarising. Not only did these two behaviours create the shared clarity that is so important in any interaction, they also had a very positive impact on the relationship between David and his client.

I too had the benefit of watching David in action. What I saw was an individual who listened carefully, checked his understanding, and took nothing for granted. More than that, when he was working, be it with an individual or a group, he was constantly looking out for signs of confusion or indications that people might have different understandings. This ability to 'watch, sense and test' is a vital skill for effective interactions.

4. Encourage participation

Meetings comprise many different types of people, often with diverse and sometimes conflicting objectives and agendas. In a typical meeting the airtime will be variously distributed across all the attendees.

Some meetings attract a type of person I've nicknamed the "passenger": the individual whose 'presence' (whether they're physically attending the meeting, at the end of the phone or part of a video conference) is not apparent in their behaviour. You can no doubt easily recall people who have been on their phones or tablets whilst in meetings. And their claims of: *"I am listening, really"* just don't cut the mustard, since the brain is incapable of multi-tasking effectively (Ralph et al). What's even more alarming is that the people who claim they are good at multi-tasking have been shown to be the worst at it (Ophir et al). So, the jugglers are just jesting. The reality is that they are there for the ride and cannot contribute effectively.

Culturally diverse groups, too, often suffer from imbalanced contributions. Oftentimes side conversations will occur as one member of the meeting tries to discuss something with another in order to better understand or express an opinion.

A smart Chair will notice who is 'in' or 'out' of the discussion and will manage the involvement of all meeting members. Equally, an effective team member can foster participation across the group in different ways, for example: by giving space so that others can speak, using an electronic whiteboard for brainstorming to capture everyone's contributions, using online surveys in remote meetings to foster discussion, asking questions and leaving space for answers.

If you're managing a meeting, there are ways you can ensure the airtime is more evenly distributed across the group. Two behaviours in particular help with managing involvement and participation in a group: **Shutting Out** and **Bringing In.**

> ***Shutting out:*** Behaving in such a way that prevents or stops another's contribution, most typically by interrupting someone.

Shutting Out is a 'Process' behaviour, relating to how the airtime in a meeting is managed. It always occurs in conjunction with another behaviour. When a Chair shuts out she speaks over another person in the meeting and interrupts their contribution. In doing so she is using Shutting Out (plus another behaviour), as these examples show:

Ann: "I suggest we..." (Incomplete proposal)

Carol: (Shutting Out and Seeking Information) "What time are we due to finish?"

Ann: "4pm. So we have time to..." *(Giving Information)*

Carol: (Shutting Out and Proposing Procedure) "Well, in that case I'll just take a short break to make a call."

When we've asked people to describe meetings that were either high or low in Shutting Out, we've had some interesting responses. Meetings where the Shutting Out level was judged to be high were commonly described as: chaotic, disorganised, frustrating, confusing, rude. As one client put it: "My head hurts!" In contrast, meetings where the Shutting Out level was rated as low were described as: slow, tortuous, boring, painful, overly polite. Or as another client said: "It's like watching paint dry."

The Chair has to strike a balance between too much and too little Shutting Out, managing the airtime in the group by shutting out unhelpfully talkative people and curbing excessive energy. The Chair also has to resist the temptation to shut out in order to add their own opinion and ideas.

As mentioned in Chapter 1, none of the 15 behaviours is in and of itself either good or bad. It's about what is *appropriate*. For example, in a board meeting where a standard part of the agenda is reporting (Giving Information) you would expect to see lower levels of Shutting Out.

I have worked with people who have an expertly judged sense of timing and can grasp a split second opportunity to get into the conversation without needing to use Shutting Out behaviours. At the other end of the spectrum are people who attempt to shut out but who don't succeed, rendering their contributions ineffective. To

Shut Out well means to Shut Out cleanly and successfully. This is an important skill for you to use in your interactions, particularly when chairing or managing meetings. Given the constraints and pressure of time, you need to exercise some control in order to effectively manage the conversation. Like most things worth doing, this ability is not easily achieved and benefits from practice.

> **Bringing in:** Seeking a contribution from a person who has not contributed for some time, or at all.

Like Shutting Out, Bringing In is a process behaviour that must be used in conjunction with another category. Strictly speaking, to bring someone 'in' to the discussion means they have to have been 'out' for a while. In other words, the individual will not have spoken for some time. Here are some examples of Bringing In:

"Sarah, what do you think?" (Seeking Information)

"What ideas do you have, Oscar?" (Seeking Proposals)

"I'd like to hear from Bart: what do you think about this?"
(Seeking Information)

"Margaux, can you summarise for us please?" (Proposing Procedure)

If you're worried about people disengaging, Bringing In can be your best friend. With a more introverted team it can be helpful not to put members on the spot but rather to create a process that gives everyone the opportunity to contribute with some advance warning. The 'Round' can be a useful intervention for managing participation. For example, a Chair might say: "Can we just take a few moments to go round the group and take any comments or questions? Dirk, can I start with you?"

> *Laurens, a young South African, had moved to Malaysia to lead a team. The culture was very respectful of hierarchy and the team*

> members said very little in meetings, expecting to be directed by Laurens. However, Laurens was conscious of the expertise in the team and wanted to ensure that this was leveraged in the best way for the business. In his meetings he would prepare his team so that they understood that he expected them to contribute. For example, he would say: "In a few moments, after I've explained some of the options for how we adopt continuous improvement, I'll ask you to discuss with the person next to you and decide two arguments for and against each option plus an additional option that has been overlooked" (Proposing Procedure). He would then go to each person in turn, bringing them in to the conversation.

Some people value time to think in interactions, welcoming an opportunity to reflect on what is being discussed. Managing participation as Laurens did in the example above can be particularly useful in providing people with the space to think before seeking their contributions.

Through skilfully managing the airtime you can ensure you get valuable input from all meeting attendees. By helping people remain engaged, you increase their investment in the subject matter under discussion and reduce the chance they'll leave the meeting with things unsaid.

Don't rely on the Chair

Although each of these four strategies can be positively influenced by the effectiveness of the Chair, any member of a high performing team will be able to execute these strategies skilfully. You may find yourself in a meeting where the Chair's ability to manage the meeting leaves a lot to be desired. In this instance, you have the opportunity to support the Chair, successfully involving the attendees and guiding the meeting to its conclusion.

Summary of key points

- Agree on a Chairperson or meetings manager

- Manage the balance of task and process

- Use process and exit surveys and learn from them

- Have the Chair or meetings manager concentrate on process through:

    - Structure: Proposing Procedure and Summarising

    - Clarity: Testing Understanding and Summarising

    - Participation: Shutting Out and Bringing In

- If you are the Chair, decide how to manage your content contributions

- If the Chair is absent or ineffective, identify how you can contribute to the meeting's effectiveness

CHAPTER 4
Establishing Your Presence

"Presence is more than just being there."

Malcolm Forbes

During my time at PricewaterhouseCoopers (PwC) I was fortunate enough to work with Peter Hawkins, now Professor of Leadership at Henley Business School. His work at PwC included helping the partners and directors of the consulting practice develop their Authority, Presence and Impact: how they could use their personal power more effectively in interactions.

What struck me at the time was how many of my peers had doubts about their ability to perform well, either as leaders of people in the practice or as client relationship managers. And this uncertainty was often evidenced in their behaviour. This self-doubt seemed to resonate in particular with my female colleagues, whose values around work were not always aligned with those of their male counterparts and whose more reticent behaviour often put them at a disadvantage. They also lacked role models of successful senior women with whom they could identify. As there was no one they could point to and say: "I want to be as good as her", they had to navigate their own way across challenging terrain.

This hesitancy was also true for some of the guys. Many of these were 'gurus' who'd risen up the ranks because of their technical expertise but who now felt challenged by the additional leadership demands being heaped upon them.

Both groups – female managers and male 'gurus' (and of course the gender split wasn't exclusive) – found that operating in a world of (apparently) confident co-workers compromised their ability to **have a voice** and **be heard**. (It bears emphasis that these are two different things.)

The reluctance to contribute can be especially true for more junior people in an organisation. Whilst confident in their day-to-day work they can appear hesitant in some interactions, particularly when their boss is present.

> *Take Sophie, for example – a trainee accountant in a professional services business. I was working with her as part of a team introducing new ways of working into the business. It became clear very early on that Sophie was an extremely bright and perceptive young woman. She would share observations with me in our conversations that demonstrated a high level of awareness about how the group was working and what would help them move forward. But when I asked Sophie about her willingness to share her insights with the group she looked very uncomfortable. Her fear of what others might think was holding her back. "I worry that others won't listen or that they might not agree with me," she told me. We explored the beliefs that were driving her behaviour and then*

practised the behavioural skills that would help her both establish her presence and develop more confidence in these interactions.

Establishing your presence comes from finding your voice and being heard, no matter where you are in the organisational hierarchy. It's essential for leaders and valuable for aspiring leaders. Finding a voice means having a point of view or perspective. Being heard means creating the conditions where you can make a contribution which people hear and understand.

Behaviourally speaking, finding a voice and being heard draw on the behaviours that help you get into a conversation or team discussion and share the airtime effectively with other contributors. There are also roles you can adopt in team meetings that provide you with a low-risk entry level for making contributions.

In her work on authenticity and leadership, Professor Herminia Ibarra of INSEAD Business School maintains that our growth is governed by the extent to which we do new things. While behaving differently may be uncomfortable at first, it's through that experience that we learn who we want to become. If you're someone disinclined to dominate interactions, establishing your presence may take you out of your comfort zone. Finding your voice is the first hurdle to overcome. Then you need feedback to confirm that your input has been received and understood.

If you find you're not being heard, let alone listened to, you may be inclined to contribute less. You may also find that more and more of your business is conducted outside of meetings. Whilst this can be a helpful way to prepare people for what will be discussed in a meeting, it can also cause duplication, increasing the time you spend on the topic. As it also has the potential to create divisions, it's not an effective option. Instead you can explore how your in-meeting behaviour could have a greater impact.

But what if you don't want to get into the conversation? At some level that's fine. After all, you may not have anything to say and, let's face it, it's a blessing when people aren't speaking for the sake of it! But what are the risks attached to not establishing your presence?

We undertook some research in a utilities business where, after meetings, we asked the more talkative team members to give their reasons as to why the quieter members did not contribute as much. Here are the top three responses, in descending order:

1. Perhaps I spoke too much

2. Maybe s/he didn't have anything to say

3. It's hard to know what s/he is thinking

We can applaud the insight in the first comment (and we can also ask why the talkative people didn't act on this in the moment!). The second and third comments are more worrying. What if you were one of those quieter contributors? What if you did have something you wanted to say? What might be the impact of people trying to second-guess what you're thinking? How might others feel about your lack of contribution? It's not what you're saying that causes concern, rather it's what you're *not* saying.

Being heard often comes down to being able to get into a discussion that's dominated by other members of the group. Timing is everything. Some people seem to have some innate, expert timing system that enables them to seize that split second when nobody is talking to jump into the conversation. However, that's not the case for most of us.

Sometimes it's enough to talk over someone in order to take control of the airtime. In other instances you may find yourself repeatedly trying to 'shut out' but just not getting your voice heard. As my colleague Robbie Macpherson once said: "You've got to get in to shut out."

The ABC Model

If this struggle to be heard chimes with you, here's a simple and brilliantly effective way of being heard and establishing your presence. I call it the 'ABC model', and it has three steps:

A *non-verbal indication*

Behaviour labelling

Category of behaviour

We'll look at each of these steps in turn.

A non-verbal indication

This is a physical signal that you want to get into the conversation. It could be leaning forward into the discussion or gesturing with your hand/arm that you want to come in. You might catch the eye of the Chair and nod to a member of your team to convey you want to contribute. These gestures send the message "I'd like to get in" or "I have something to say".

Behaviour labelling

A behaviour label announces the behaviour that is going to follow. For example: "Can I just make a suggestion?" flags that a proposal is imminent. "If I could just come in here with some additional information…" tells the audience that you're about to Give Information.

The value of labelling is that it signals to those present that there's more to come and that you need the airtime. It can also slow the discussion down. When behaviour labelling is used there's much less shutting out from other people in the discussion. In other words, you're more likely to keep the airtime if you've announced you have a contribution to make. People who label behaviour are judged to be more effective than others.

There is one exception to this rule – labelling a disagreement. For example: "I'd like to tell you why your idea won't work" or "No, no, no, I disagree because..." Rackham hypothesised that a labelled disagreement happens because your brain makes an immediate decision along the lines of "that's not right", and later you use your rational thinking to give your reasons for disagreeing. "Decide first, justify later". This is in contrast to analytical decision-making, which results in slower processing. Rackham's hypothesis is borne out by Daniel Kahneman's inspirational work on system 1 and 2 thinking.

Stop and think for a moment. If you're in a conversation and someone announces they disagree with you, what are you most likely to do next? All our experience suggests that most people would immediately focus on their own counter-arguments, explaining why their own ideas will work and why the dissenter is wrong rather than listening to the reasons for disagreement. In short, labelling disagreement leads to a communications shutdown and should be avoided where possible. (You can read more about Disagreeing in Chapter 6 – 'Reacting Behaviours'.)

Category of behaviour

The category of behaviour you select depends on what you want to say. For example, if you have an idea you want to share you will use one of the initiating behaviours: Proposing Procedure, Proposing Content, or Building. It might sound like: "If I could just come in here with a suggestion (label), we could take a break now whilst the presenters are setting up and reconvene in ten minutes" (Proposing Procedure).

It's not just the quieter contributors who can benefit from the ABC model. If you are a more talkative person, you too can also increase your chances of being listened to by exercising some control over your behaviours. For example:

- If you are Shutting Out, do so cleanly and effectively, using the A, B, C model
- Get in, say what you want to say (succinctly) and get out

How airtime is shared

In group interactions that are working well we observe the spread of airtime between the highest contributor and the lowest contributor to be at a rough ratio of 3:1. This means that if the most talkative person makes 90 contributions in an hour-long meeting, the least talkative would be making around 30 contributions. While the ratio may change according to the purpose of the meeting, this is a useful rule of thumb for ensuring everyone has the opportunity to have their say. Research undertaken at Google found that 'good' teams had "equality in the distribution of conversational turn-taking", with each team member having more or less the same proportion of airtime.

Sharing the airtime data can be very revealing. While it's true that some groups have a good level of awareness about who is doing most of the talking, I've worked with many groups whose members were genuinely surprised (and often embarrassed) when the airtime figures were revealed. Here is an example from a training programme. The data comes from two groups from the same organisation. Each group worked independently in an idea-generating session designed to address the same business problem. Their data is displayed as the total number of contributions per person in each team.

	GROUP 1		GROUP 2
Jan	145	Stephanie	75
Paul	103	Dominic	74
Simon	101	Anna	70
Pieter	34	Laura	65
Grace	26	Alex	56
Joyce	7	Kevin	35
	416		375

Fig 13. Sharing Airtime

What do you notice about each group?

What do you imagine it's like to be Joyce in Group 1?

How might people feel about Jan in Group 1?

Which group do you imagine was most effective?

Of course, you have to be there to really understand what happened and the impact of these behaviours. Nonetheless, the raw data prompts some useful questions for reflection.

> On one occasion, when I was working with a multi-disciplinary, multi-cultural group, the airtime scores revealed Dana topping the charts with 532 contributions and Mo notching up just 6. This disparity in contributions opened up a treasure trove of learning opportunities for the group. Mo expressed his frustration at not being able to get into the conversation, despite the fact he had much he wanted to contribute. Having shared this, the group took on a collective responsibility to bring him in. Mo also practised and perfected the use of the ABC model to turn up the dial on the impact of his contributions.

How quieter members can contribute

You may be reluctant to contribute to some discussions, especially if you feel it's just for the sake of appearances. However, there are some behaviours that lower contributors can use that are of value to everyone in the discussion. The two most positive value-adding behaviours are:

1. **Summarising.** If you're sitting quietly in a meeting you have the ability to listen to what is being discussed and then share a synopsis with the group. Your contribution will help to establish clarity, avoid any misunderstandings, get everyone to the same stage of the journey and identify what more needs to be discussed.

2. **Seeking Information.** As you listen to the conversation you can help the group explore what's being discussed through the skilful use of questioning. The behavioural budget of most groups is over-spent on Giving Information, so you can redress the balance through exercising your curiosity.

Contributing through roles

In teamwork there are roles that you can adopt that help increase your contribution while also enhancing the effectiveness the group. Four roles are particularly useful:

Timekeeper

Minute-taker

Scribe

Bridger

1. Timekeeper

The timekeeper helps the group stay on track in relation to their original itinerary while adapting the timings when the route needs to change. It sounds so simple but it's a role that is often neglected and its absence can result in the timing of the agenda in meetings going 'to pot'. Furthermore, having the watch means the timekeeper can raise the group's level of awareness about just how much time is being used. For example: "Just to let you know, we have spent 25 minutes discussing this topic against our planned 15. What would you like to do?" (Giving Information and Seeking Proposals).

2. Minute-taker

The Minute-taker adopts a traditional but surprisingly overlooked role: that of documenting an accurate record what has been discussed and agreed. This role requires good listening skills, the ability to use Testing Understanding and Seeking Information to ensure that what you have heard is both correct and accurately represented, and the ability to Summarise to ensure that all the points have been captured before the discussion moves on to the next item. This can be a helpful role to adopt if you're new to the team, since you can learn a lot about how the team works and the content of the work itself *and* you can make a valuable contribution from a position of relative ignorance.

3. Scribe

The Scribe is the individual who leaps up to the flip chart to record what is being discussed and agreed. Making the key points and actions visible on the flip chart makes a big contribution to driving up the level of clarity in the meeting, thereby helping to keep the discussion focussed. Like the Minute-taker, the Scribe requires good listening skills and ability in the behaviours of Testing Understanding, Seeking Information and Summarising.

4. Bridger

The Bridger is a highly skilled role. To be a Bridger you need to know the team's strengths and weaknesses. What is the team good at? What type of work do the team members prefer to do? Where are there gaps? The Bridger helps by directing team members to areas where they have strong preferences or where they've expressed a development need. The Bridger will also know where the gaps are in the team and suggest ways for plugging them by involving others or by taking responsibility to fill the gap. The Team Management Profile (Margerison and McCann) is an excellent tool for establishing and understanding preferences in a team. Their questionnaire establishes an individual's work preferences across four measures. These are combined with their research-based Types of Work Model, which identifies eight types of work that are always present in high-performing teams. The resulting profile explores the breadth and complexity of the individual's work preferences and the impact this can have on the role they play in a team as well as their leadership style. A Bridger is alert to those preferences and draws on them to fill gaps in the team, thereby avoiding or mitigating potential problems. In engaging with the team the Bridger will be using a range of the 15 behaviour categories.

Bad habits

We can all get into some 'bad' or unhelpful behavioural habits. The behaviour you use at work is no exception and sometimes your behaviour undermines your presence. There is one habit in particular to be aware of: what Rackham and Carlisle call an 'Irritator'. An Irritator is a behaviour, which if frequently used, can cause others to become irritated.

> *Frank, a senior manager in an international bank, repeatedly used the phrase "To be frank..." (meaning "to be honest") during*

his negotiations with clients. Whilst at one level this might have been amusing (given his name was Frank), the behaviour had two unhelpful consequences. First, its repeated use served to irritate the other party. Secondly, the client began to wonder if Frank was sometimes not being honest.

Kirsty had recently joined the board of a consulting business. It was her first board role and she had much to learn about the business and the role of being on the board. In meetings she was frequently heard to apologise for her apparent shortcomings. The overuse of "I'm sorry" meant her behaviour no longer conveyed the positive message that she was willing to learn. Instead the repeated apologies only served to undermine her presence and hinder her effectiveness in entering this new arena.

It's easy to spot the irritator in others. One of my colleagues repeatedly uses the phrase "In any shape or form". I have a Belgian client who prefaces everything he says with "Allez!" (and he doesn't mean my name!). Sharing the impact of these behaviours can be useful feedback for your colleagues, especially if you can help them find alternative ways of expressing themselves. Spotting your own irritators isn't so easy, so be sure to ask others if you have them and consider what you can do about them.

When establishing your presence, the ABC model is a useful guide as to how to get into a conversation. In addition, the four roles of Timekeeper, Minute-taker, Scribe and Bridger provide ways to contribute actively and skilfully. It can also be helpful for the group to agree some rules of operation. For example, some groups establish a 'no interruptions' rule for parts of their discussion to ensure everyone has time to speak.

I've also seen groups use the 'Talking Stick' to good effect. The origins of the talking stick lie in Aboriginal culture. The practice denotes that speaking is linked to possession of the stick, so that you can only talk when you're the one holding the stick. Not only does this help give everyone an opportunity to get in but it also creates the space to really listen to what is being said. In groups where listening skills are poor I will often use the listening stick and, when it is passed to the next person, I will invite that person to summarise the points made thus far. It's remarkable how quickly people then focus on listening to others rather than on what they want to say.

Sometimes behaviour alone is not enough

Mo, the low contributor in the earlier example, was over 1.85m tall and a well-built guy. He also had a high-pitched voice that could be hard to attune to. Helen, another client, was knocking on the door for promotion to director in a professional services firm. Whilst she could get into discussions, her delivery appeared timid and gave the impression of lacking in confidence. Using the tactics outlined in this chapter, both Mo and Helen made significant progress – but it wasn't enough. They supplemented their increased behavioural know-how by working with a voice coach who helped them improve the delivery of each behaviour. Their contributions increased in impact as they were able to establish a presence and hold the attention of the other team members. Working with actors, too, can help people in the business world communicate with greater authority, presence and impact.

Summary of key points

- Prioritise getting into the discussion to establish your presence

- Get into discussions effectively by using the 'ABC model', with its three steps: **A** non-verbal indication; **B**ehaviour labelling; and **C**ategory of behaviour

- Behaviour labelling is highly correlated with successful performers, with the exception of labelling disagreement

- Monitor and manage how you are contributing to the airtime, remembering the 3:1 ratio

- Contribute through the use of behaviours that help the group: Seeking Information and Summarising

- Contribute through roles that help the group: Timekeeper, Minute-taker, Scribe, Bridger

- Know your own irritators as well as those of others and collaborate to overcome them

- If necessary, use other resources, like a voice coach or an actor, to help maximise the impact of your behavioural delivery

CHAPTER 5
Fostering Creativity

"Enlightened trial and error succeeds over the planning of the lone genius."

Peter Skillman (formerly of IDEO)

Creativity is the use of imagination or original ideas to create something new and seeing connections between things that already exist. In business, creativity gets mixed reactions. It can be embraced enthusiastically as a means for opening up new possibilities. Equally it can be judged with suspicion because many people are resistant to change.

From an evolutionary perspective, humans have needed creativity for survival. As a species we've had to be flexible enough to deal with whatever has crossed our path. As the saying goes: "Necessity is the mother of invention." We've had to create and adapt to survive.

In our sophisticated world today, creativity is essential to the performance and longevity of business. Together with innovation, creativity is the lifeblood of organisations. If you keep doing what you've always done, eventually no one will want it. The responsibility to generate and shape ideas doesn't just rest with functions that are labelled 'R&D' or 'Innovation' or 'Marketing'. Every function and every role in business carries with it the scope and the responsibility to create and style ideas. No one is excluded.

Being creative combines different capabilities in your brain, activating different systems.

In generating ideas you draw on divergent thinking. In selecting between ideas you draw on your decision-making abilities. We'll look at both these stages of creativity, together with the behaviours that best support each stage. But first we will turn our attention to the factors that limit your creativity.

What limits creativity?

Our work in many different businesses has revealed four main reasons why creativity is constrained:

Competition

Dominance

Lack of resourcefulness

Self-regulation

We'll now look at each of these in turn.

1. Competition

People compete for ideas: "my idea's better than yours". At the point where you wed yourself to your own solution you stop listening to others. No longer open to further possibilities, you fail to harness the wisdom of the many. Behaviourally, the likely sequence you'll hear is Proposing Content, then a counter Content Proposal, followed by a series of exchanges using Giving Information to explain why my idea is indeed better than yours. Positions are adopted and the opportunity to explore and shape the ideas is lost. This happens a lot with 'experts'. Individuals make a commitment to an idea and are reluctant to explore alternative options. Instead they engage in intellectual argument to justify their position.

2. Dominance

Someone in the group dominates. It could be a leader who uses their authority to railroad the group or it could be a powerful personality with the drive of a runaway train. Stealing the airtime in this way means there are limited opportunities for others to contribute, no matter how willing or able. Behaviourally, you'll hear Proposing Content followed by Giving Information. If you're the person wanting to 'get into' the discussion, remember the tips we explored for that in the previous chapter.

3. Lack of resourcefulness

It's hard to be creative on demand. Sandwiching business that requires creative thinking into an agenda otherwise full of factual reporting is likely to reap fewer ideas than a session that creates the optimum conditions for creativity. Behaviourally, you've been drowned in a sea of Giving Information and it's hard enough to keep your head above water without the added pressure to generate ideas.

Some personality types find idea generation harder than others. If you're the boss or chairing a meeting, knowing your people's preferences means you can reinforce the creativity quotient by 'renting in' people who enjoy this type of work.

4. Self-regulation

When you're regulating yourself you're less likely to be creative because your brain is hearing the instruction "Don't": "Don't do this", "Don't say anything." This often results from a sense of low psychological safety. When you feel psychologically safe you're able to show yourself, and indeed 'be' yourself, without fear of negative consequences. This is not always easy at work where you can be in competition with others, where judgments are made about you and where some bosses can have a reputation for being critical.

The team leader has a responsibility to create an environment that is ripe for creativity. This includes helping team members to engage in behaviourally helpful ways. For creativity to flow, people need to feel psychologically safe and that failure is OK. You can help others feel safe by valuing their contributions and withholding judgment. Behaviourally, you can do this through Bringing In, Seeking Information, Support and Building.

Creating the conditions for creativity

There's well-documented research on the impact the environment has on creativity (for example, the work of Professor Juliet Zhu). It's not my intention to repeat the many research findings here, merely to highlight some key points:

- Getting your brain into a relaxed state leaves it free to explore possibilities

- Having skill and confidence will help you to get into the 'flow', a concept defined by the psychologist Mihaly Csikszentmihalyi, which is evidenced by complete absorption in what you're doing

- Different types of sensory and cognitive input will feed your brain, as when you play music. An example is the growing tendency of businesses to invite people from different spheres to participate in idea generation and problem-solving sessions. A power company might involve a boat-maker, a potter and a teacher in a problem-solving session in order to gain different perspectives. This can result in what Frans Johansson describes as 'The Medici Effect' – the power of innovation when diverse disciplines and ideas collide.

- Create intervals of rest: the most novel ideas tend to emerge after periods of incubation where the brain does its connecting and other-than-conscious processing.

One of my colleagues also refers to the importance of 'Place', meaning a change to an entirely different environment to stimulate creativity.

The Disney organisation is renowned for a creative strategy which provides distinct space for the different stages of creativity and which bridges the gap between imagination and reality. In a room, or in separate rooms, clearly-defined areas are marked out for each stage of the process:

1. **The Creative** – where ideas are imagined and accepted (Seeking Proposals, Proposing Content and Building)

2. **The Realist** – where ideas are translated into plans (Seeking Information and Testing Understanding, Proposing Content and Building)

3. **The Critic** – where barriers to implanting ideas are identified and overcome (Seeking Information, Testing Understanding, Disagreeing, Supporting, Seeking Proposals, Building)

A client of mine was exploring how to embed best practice in day-to-day work in their global business. One of the ideas that gained traction was to create an 'aquarium' on each site. This was a metaphor for a resource space where people came together to share ideas and learn. The idea sprang from the fact they'd been on a learning and development programme and wanted to continue the theme of learning, which they likened to swimming in the waters of an aquarium. It didn't require any resources to implement, simply the will to create a space for learning.

Generating ideas

The process of coming up with ideas requires divergent thinking – spontaneous, free-flowing thought, capable of producing creative ideas. The principal behaviours used here are Initiating behaviours: **Proposing Content** and **Building**.

1. Proposing Content

Definition: Suggesting a new concept or idea that is actionable and relates to the subject matter under discussion.

For example, at a meeting to come up with ideas for the office Christmas party, examples of Content Proposals would be:

> "What about a fancy dress party?" (Proposing Content in the form of a question)

> "Let's have a children's tea party and invite families."

> "We could have a safari meal, with each course of the meal in a different restaurant."

> "What about a disco at the local hotel?"

In generating ideas the focus is on quantity rather than quality. Brainstorming is the most commonly used technique. For introverts it helps to have some post-it notes prior to starting a brainstorm. This gives a short period of time for reflection, for thinking of ideas by yourself before contributing out loud. Post-it notes are also a good way to control the verbal flow of the extroverts so that you get time to think.

It's useful to remind people of the rules of brainstorming which are often observed in the breach. The three basic rules are:

- **Quantity not quality**

- **Anything goes**

- **Defer judgment**

I work with a number of organisations whose employees include some fiercely analytical people. In brainstorming sessions they have a tendency to pause when an idea comes up and start to evaluate it. Or they might immediately react to an idea and (usually) say why it won't work. This is the kiss of death to any ideas-generation session. Remember: the behavioural focus is on Proposing Content and Building – the Initiating behaviours. There will be some Clarifying but little or no Reacting. When group members start to use other behaviours you might consider invoking a 'red card' to draw attention to the unhelpful behaviours. You could also use a bell or a rattle – anything that alerts people to the fact they've drifted off course.

Research by Dr Tony McCaffrey advocates the use of 'Brainswarming', a method which encourages individuals to generate ideas on their own and jot them down on post-it notes before sharing them with the group. The method works for both top-down and bottom-up thinkers and can help give everyone time to think. It's also useful for managing the spread of airtime.

For adults, it's much harder to be creative unless you first inhibit the ordinary or the habitual. In other words, to maximise your creativity you have to get past the obvious. For example, after brainstorming some ideas you can pose certain questions to the group (Seeking Proposals):

"If you were to ignore all those ideas, what else could you do?"

"What ideas would (insert the name of someone) come up with?"

"How would an (engineer/ballet dancer, etc.) respond to this?"

The additional phase of Seeking Proposals provokes people to extend their thinking and push past the familiar.

2. Building

Definition: Extending or developing a proposal which has been made by another person.

Building does what it says – it builds on an existing proposal. It's a highly effective behaviour, and a rare one, since it demands you listen to other people's contributions, resisting the temptation to be consumed by your own ideas. It also requires you to be agile at processing all the ideas that are being generated. The great news is that, like all behaviour, Building can be learned. It's simply a matter of practice and feedback.

Building is strongly correlated with skilled performers (Rackham and Morgan). The impact of Building is that others feel listened to and the climate in the session is perceived as positive. Neurologically Building causes a dopamine hit: "People like my idea". Building also creates momentum. When you're in an ideas-generating session and it feels like you're really motoring, it's often because someone or some people are using Building behaviour.

If we go back to generating ideas for the office Christmas party, we can take one of the Content Proposals:

> "Let's have a children's tea party and invite families…"

and we can build on that:

> "Yes! And we could have jelly and ice cream…"

> "And sprinkles…"

> "And we could play pin the tail on the donkey…"

> "Or on the MD!"

You can almost hear the momentum with the "Yes, and…" intention of a Build.

Building can help you to get past the obvious, too. For example, you can take any of the proposals you've generated and ask people (Seeking Builds):

> "And what are two ways in which we could make this idea (even) more wacky?"

> "What are three ways in which we can make this idea even stronger?"

You can also invite people to select different proposals and generate their own Builds. The value here is that you get to focus on Building behaviour alone and, through that concentrated practice, get into the habit of Building. Hence (pardon the pun) you can build that muscle!

A final comment on generating ideas: my experience is that teams do a better job of this when they're standing up rather than seated. There's something about sitting around a table that restricts the energy needed for developing new ideas. It's useful to think about how you can create the space for movement.

Formalising a break after creating ideas and before evaluating those ideas helps sustain the goodwill that has been generated, creates time for reflection and allows the brain to do its other-than-conscious work.

Evaluating and selecting ideas

Moving into evaluation and selection requires more process and participation management (Proposing Procedure, Bringing In and Shutting Out). In evaluating and selecting ideas the first step is to remove any duplicates. Sometimes it's useful to cluster the remaining ideas together.

Evaluation can be done in a number of ways. The two most frequently used are:

1. Evaluating each idea against some agreed criteria (Seeking Information, Disagreeing and Supporting). Identifying these criteria may also be another opportunity for brainstorming (Seeking Proposals, Content Proposals and Building)

2. Voting for the most preferred or the three best options (Giving Information)

I've found that groups often produce some of their best work when they also take time to consider the least favoured options. One way of doing this is to use the **Power of Three:** for example, invite members of the group to give three reasons why this is a valuable idea (Giving Information) or make three suggestions that will increase the power of this idea (Building). The Power of Three is also a helpful way to push past the obvious.

When evaluating ideas you may find yourself feeling more and more committed to one idea rather than any other. It can be helpful to pause and ask yourself the question: "I wonder why that is?" To best serve the group, wherever possible try to defer judgment and use your skills of Seeking Information and Testing Understanding to help everyone exhaust their evaluative stores.

Summary of key points

- Creativity is essential for survival

- Being creative activates different parts of the brain

- Creativity can be constrained by competition, dominance, lack of resourcefulness, and self-regulation

- Creating a sense of psychological safety enhances creativity and positively impacts performance

- Paying attention to the environment optimises the conditions for creativity

- Generating ideas is driven by Seeking Proposals, Proposing Content and Building

- Pushing past the obvious is vital and can be achieved by Seeking Proposals and Building

- Building, a rare and powerful skill, needs to be integrated into your process

- Using the Power of Three can help extend your ideas

- Focusing on Seeking Information and Testing Understanding is helpful when evaluating and selecting ideas

CHAPTER 6
Reacting

"There is more hunger for love and appreciation in this world than for bread."

Mother Teresa

When you're working with ideas or sharing facts and opinions, people invariably respond to what you are saying. Certain behaviours reveal how an individual is reacting to other contributions – and to the people making those contributions. These are commonly known as the 'Reacting' behaviours, and there are three of them:

Supporting

Disagreeing

Defending-Attacking

1. Supporting

Definition: A clear, unambiguous statement of support for, or agreement with, another contribution or a person. Examples are:

> "I really like that idea, Sonja."

> "Peter, what you have just explained has been very helpful."

> "Joanna has done some excellent work on this topic."

> "Thank you, Jon, for agreeing to capture the points."

2. Disagreeing

Definition: Making a clear statement of disagreement with someone else's statement, opinion, idea or approach, or raising objections to a contribution:

> "That will never work."

> "I would describe it differently."

> "I think that could be too hard for the trainees"

> "Absolutely not!"

> "I'm not sure I see it that way."

3. Defending-Attacking

Definition: Showing an emotional 'attack' on another person in the interaction, or an emotional 'defence':

> "The trouble with you IT folks is that you just don't understand about budgets!"

"You've got a cheek saying that my handwriting is illegible. What does that make yours?"

"Don't be so ridiculous!"

"Can you stop picking on me?"

Reacting behaviours are fundamental to our daily interactions. They can be helpful in letting other people know where we're coming from and provide a means of feedback on ideas and information. Using these behaviours means that people don't have to second-guess what we're thinking. Reacting behaviours also play a key role in group decision-making.

Supporting as a behaviour activates the reward system in the brain, releasing the chemical dopamine and creating a feel-good factor. If you get random, intermittent positive reinforcement you're more likely to repeat that behaviour. Disagreeing and Defending-Attacking can trigger the amygdala to perceive a threat. Your brain is constantly assessing how much reward or threat there is in a given situation, and your emotional calibration in those situations depends on the emotions you've previously experienced. If you get a huge kick from your amygdala, your hippocampus (the filing cabinet of the brain) says "that's worth remembering". I often liken the relationship between the two circuits in this way: activating the reward circuit is akin to the 'pip' of a fairy light coming on in the brain; the impact on the brain is transitory. In contrast, triggering the threat circuit is like switching on the illuminations at the Eiffel Tower, a 'BLAHH!' And the impact is longer lasting.

THREAT   **REWARD**

Fig 14. The Impact of Threat and Reward

In spite of increased awareness of the value of emotional intelligence in the business world, most people I work with tend not to be aware of the reacting style they have, nor its impact.

You may be someone who reacts slowly. The upside of this is that you're less likely to make a faux pas or rush into things. The downside is that people may find it hard to know where you stand. On the other hand, you may be someone who reacts more quickly, clearly signaling your position. In doing do you may inhibit further discussion, particularly if you're the boss.

Most of our behaviour is unconscious. One of the values of Behaviour Analysis is that it helps you to be conscious of what you do and say and the impact of your behaviours on others. When given a snapshot of your behaviour you can see what you actually did rather than what you thought you did, and this includes learning about your reacting style.

CHAPTER 6

Rackham and Morgan's research on Reacting behaviours suggests that, ideally, Supporting and Disagreeing should absorb 10-20% of an individual's behavioural budget. The research also recommends that these two behaviours should be *in balance:* in other words, they should score around the same. If your levels for both behaviours are below or above that range, you can make a conscious choice to behave differently, if that's appropriate.

Reacting behaviours come in all manner of frequencies. We've all come across people who seem to react often and seemingly without thinking, in contrast to others who give little or no reaction. Some people will emphasise the negatives, flexing their Disagreeing muscle. Others always look for the positives and major on Supporting. The diagram below illustrates the possible combinations of Supporting and Disagreeing behaviours.

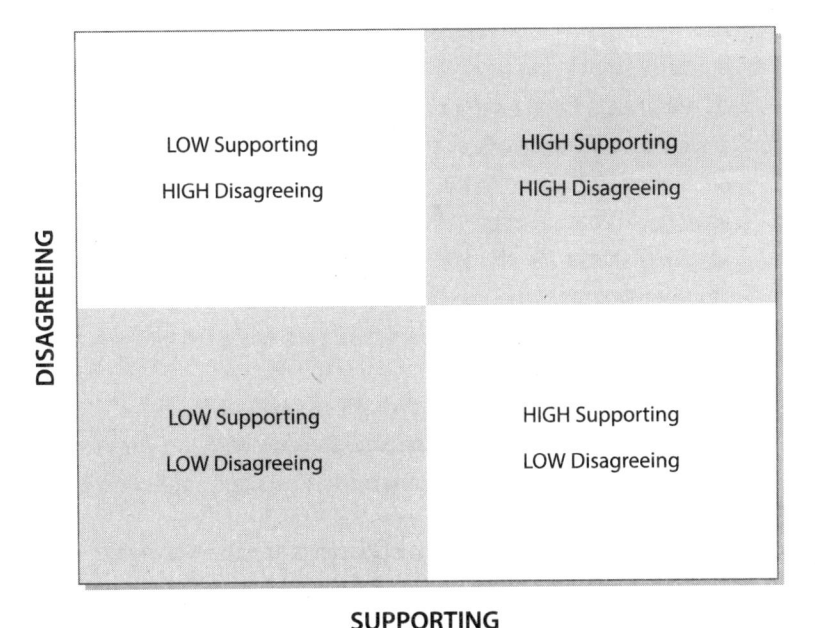

LOW Supporting HIGH Disagreeing	HIGH Supporting HIGH Disagreeing
LOW Supporting LOW Disagreeing	HIGH Supporting LOW Disagreeing

DISAGREEING (y-axis) / **SUPPORTING** (x-axis)

Fig 15. Supporting and Disagreeing

Low Supporting and Low Disagreeing

Rackham labelled a person with Low Supporting and Low Disagreeing as a 'Low Reactor'. A Low Reactor spends less than 10% of their behavioural budget on reacting behaviours. Being a Low Reactor doesn't mean you're a lower contributor, it simply means that you're sparing with your use of Supporting and Disagreeing behaviours. Most people who meet this descriptor are unaware of their reacting style and therefore unaware of the impact it can have on others.

> *During my early days as a consultant, I pitched a piece of work to a client. I'd been really thorough in my preparation, even to the point of rehearsing and asking my colleagues to put me through my paces with the kind of killer questions a client might ask. I felt confident, but not cocky. I was really looking forward to the pitch. When I arrived at the client's office my contact announced that the new Procurement Director was going to be joining us. I saw this as a positive move and thought no more of it. Then I started my pitch. I'd designed it to be interactive so the client could get a feel of what it would be like to work with me. As I got into my stride I became acutely aware of the blank face of the Procurement Director. He gave no visible signs of liking or rejecting what I had to say. As I got further into my story I allowed myself to be distracted by him. Beginning to feel anxious, I tripped over my words. In short, what had started off, at least in theory, as a well-designed pitch ended up as an inarticulate disaster.*
>
> *I had fallen into the trap of the Low Reactor. When I later learned that I was not the first to be caught out it was but small consolation.*

Some people are trained to be Low Reactors. It can be a very helpful modus operandi for negotiators and buyers. By giving nothing away in terms of their reaction levels, the Low Reactor can bring the other party or parties under their spell. In my work observing negotiations in international banking and in mergers and acquisitions I've often seen the power of the Low Reactor yielding dividends for one side or other.

> Paul was negotiating a new banking arrangement with a client – a large dairy business. The deal was potentially very valuable to the bank and would be a major coup for Paul. The client team was headed up by a gentleman who presented as a very cool character. Polite and organised, he was the picture of efficiency. He also appeared somewhat aloof. All Paul's efforts to broker a warm and friendly relationship failed to break the ice. I could see Paul beginning to question himself and starting to appear a little nervous. The client kept his distance, asking skilful questions which exposed the weakness of Paul's position as he drove for lower fees. As Paul made a concession on the fee rate the client gave no reaction. Thinking that his concession wasn't enough and desperately wanting the business, Paul made a further concession to the client, only to get nothing in return. He had fallen into the Low Reactor trap and ended up with a deal that would cost the bank dearly.

Whilst there's some merit in the likes of procurement professionals and negotiators refining the art of low reacting, what if you're a manager or a leader? The impact on your relationships with your team can be very damaging, for various reasons:

- Lack of recognition for achievement or effort

- Difficulty building rapport

- You appear detached and indifferent

- There's inherent distrust

- Your behaviour creates anxiety in others

- Decision-making gets delayed because people are uncertain of your position

And so the list goes on.

When I get into conversation with managers who are Low Reactors, a defence I often hear is: "Yes, but if I don't disagree surely people will know it's OK?" And therein lies the rub, for 'people' don't know it's OK and it could be dangerous to assume that's the case. Not reacting can also be a form of laziness on the part of managers, one that results in less behavioural flexibility and reduced effectiveness.

If you fall into the Low Reactor category, what can you do? The best place to start is to focus on more Supporting behaviour. This is because you are already likely to be judged with some suspicion or viewed as negative, and so Disagreeing or Defending-Attacking behaviours will only reinforce those views. Make a conscious effort to notice your team's work, remarking positively on their contributions, progress and results. Remember that the definition of Supporting behaviour is 'a clear statement of support or agreement'. Simply saying "Great" doesn't constitute Supporting. Instead, say things like:

"That's an excellent report, Darren."

"Well done, Sophie, we can learn a lot from your approach."

"Thank you, everyone, for your contributions."

"What I really like is the way you laid out the timeline."

Ian was a senior manager in a power company. In a 360° feedback exercise he was surprised by some of the comments which described him as 'cold' and 'unapproachable' in terms of his leadership style. Ian invited me to observe his team meeting. I collected some data and afterwards we had a conversation about how representative the meeting was. His view was that it was fairly typical. We looked at the data and in particular at Ian's reacting levels. He had spent just 3% of his behavioural budget in this area, and all of that on Disagreeing. Little wonder that his 360° comments were critical of

> his style. This was a useful place for Ian to consider building some new behavioural muscle, starting with Supporting.

If you are a Low Reactor and a low contributor, it's likely that people get conditioned to not hearing you speak. When you do make a contribution there's an increased risk that what you say may be overlooked or under-valued.

If you work with Low Reactors, the best strategy is to ask them for their reactions:

> "What do you think about that?"
>
> "How do you react to that?"
>
> "What are your thoughts?"
>
> "What do you like/dislike about it?"

It may help to let the Low Reactors know beforehand that you'll be seeking their views. This provides them with some thinking time and avoids putting them on the spot.

High Disagreeing, Low Supporting

The profile of High Disagreeing and Low Supporting surfaces less often than does that of the Low Reactor. A person with this scoring is frequently described as 'negative', 'obstructive', and 'pessimistic'. When I come across managers and team leaders with this profile, I'm curious about the impact of their reacting behaviour on their staff. Their response is often along the lines of: "Why do I need to support someone who's doing their job?"

Disagreeing without the balance of Support can result in the other person's brain threat circuitry being activated. Perhaps worse than that, ignoring or failing to notice the work that people are doing is a missed opportunity for Supporting behaviour, with all its positive implications.

Sometimes Disagreeing has an even more negative impact. This is when the Disagreeing is labelled. If you recall, labelling announces the behaviour that's coming next. The label comes first and the reasons for Disagreeing follow, as in the following:

"I don't agree with you because..."

"No, no, no, that won't work..."

"I have to disagree on that point..."

Here's an example of labelled Disagreeing from a meeting about introducing a new performance development process in a professional services firm:

Katka: *I think it would be useful if we provided all the managers with some training on the process and the paperwork.* (Proposing Content)

John: *That's a good idea* (Supporting), *and we could create some practice exercises for them to run through.* (Building)

Carlo: *I disagree. That won't work. We haven't got the resources to design and deliver the training and the managers should know what's expected of them.* (Labelled Disagreeing)

Just take a moment to read that snippet of conversation again. This time, imagine you are Katka. What are you thinking immediately after Carlo has spoken?

Fig 16. What's Katka Thinking and Feeling?

You may be thinking: "I'd like to understand why Carlo thinks that". In which case, well done for being curious. Or you may be silently irritated by Carlo's negativity. You say nothing but your irritation may well leak out later. A third response is that you've stopped listening to his reasons as to why your proposal won't work because you're focussed on preparing your rebuttal.

If you're someone given to labelling Disagreeing, it's likely you will be perceived as negative. The chances are that people may stop listening to what you're saying.

Alternatives to Disagreeing

People who are behaviourally skilled will avoid labelling Disagreeing and will sometimes select alternatives to Disagreeing. These substitute behaviours can have a less negative impact than repeated Disagreeing.

If you were to consider a spectrum of behaviours as options for Disagreeing it would look like this:

```
LOW ═══════════ SKILL LEVEL ═══════════ HIGH
  ○             ○              ○              ○              ○
Labelled    Disagreeing    Testing       Giving        Building
Disagreeing               Understanding  Feelings
```

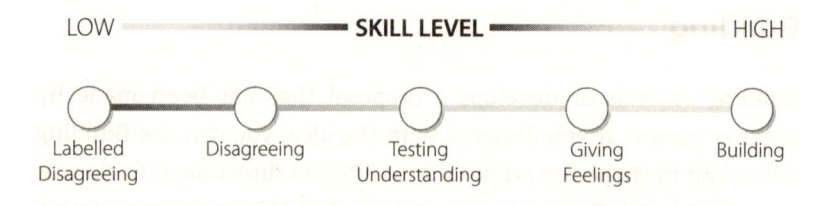

Fig 17. Behavioural Options When You Want to Disagree

As we've already explored Labelled Disagreeing and Disagreeing, let's look at the other options.

Testing Understanding

Testing Understanding can be used as an alternative to Disagreeing. In the example above Carlo could have said:

"So do you mean all 250 managers would be trained?" or

"Are you saying we should be delivering the training to all the managers?"

These questions check that Carlo has correctly understood what Katka has proposed and they could also cause Katka to re-evaluate her idea.

Giving Feelings

Giving Feelings is an expression of your feelings about what's happening in an interaction (we'll explore this behaviour further in the next chapter). If Carlo had chosen this option, he might have said something like:

"I'm feeling uncomfortable that we're focussing on just one option (Giving Feelings). *Could we brainstorm some alternatives?"* (Proposing Procedure)

Building

Building extends or develops a proposal that has been made by another person. If you disagree with the idea, you can use Building behaviour to shape the proposal in a different direction. If Carlo was disagreeing with Katka because of the lack of HR resources to design and deliver the training, a Build might sound like:

> "And because the best way to learn is to teach we could ask for volunteers from the manager cadre."

Of these three options Building is probably the most difficult because it requires Carlo to listen to what Katka is saying and then think about how best to modify her proposal. However, the payoff from using Building is likely to be greater since the behaviour is perceived as more helpful and contributes to a positive atmosphere in the meeting.

High Supporting, Low Disagreeing

I'm always curious when I see this profile. Questions that run through my head include:

> "What does this person do when s/he disagrees?"

> "What's driving this behaviour?"

> "How do other people respond?"

High Supporting behaviour can result from wanting to be seen in a favourable light. The behaviour is driven by ego. And after a while the high frequency of Supporting starts to undermine its impact.

> Cora was a manager of a sales team. Whenever anyone in the team had done something well she would respond with "Good job". This phrase was used so often that it failed to have any meaning.

> Rather than having the desired positive impact, "Good job" became a behavioural irritator and the team started to discount both the message and Cora's credibility.

If you fit the High Supporting, Low Disagreeing profile it's worth exploring why this might be. What are you seeking to achieve? What behavioural alternatives might be more productive?

If a team has this profile, this suggests 'group think' is in operation and that the drive to conform is stronger than desire for the optimum decision.

High Supporting, High Disagreeing

Where both these Reacting behaviours comprise 20% or more of spend in a person's behavioural budget you are faced with a High Reactor. Because the reacting behaviours are popping off like champagne corks at a wedding, it can be very difficult to understand where this individual is coming from. Descriptors for High Reactors include: 'fickle', 'indecisive', 'capricious', and 'woolly'. The reactions become meaningless. Instead they just add to the noise of the communication, which becomes irritating and causes people to switch off. High Reacting is also risky because the individual might be using the wrong reaction. Worse still, many people we have asked describe the High Reactor as 'not to be trusted'. Worryingly, High Reacting can also be a sign of someone under stress.

When handling a High Reactor, the best strategy is to ask them questions to test their thinking. The questioning also slows them down. Reflecting back their contributions by using Testing Understanding and Summarising enables you to help them gain some behavioural control. If you're managing and/or coaching a High Reactor it's useful to explore what's driving this behaviour, along with their options for developing more skilful interventions.

What's normal?

The sweet spot for Supporting and Disagreeing lies in-between the Low and High Reactor, where the total of the two categories of behaviour is roughly between 10-20% and in balance. If you think you fall outside of this zone you have the perfect opportunity to build and flex some new behavioural muscle.

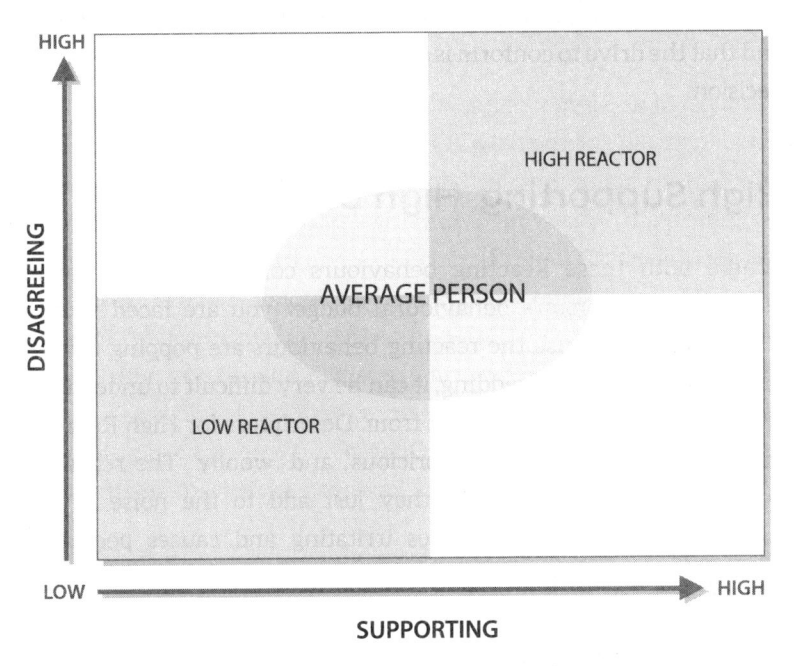

Fig 18. Reacting Behaviours

Adapted from *'Rackham: Interactive Skills'* with permission

Cultural reactions

It's true to say that some of the reacting behaviours don't travel easily across cultures. For example, it's rare to see High Disagreeing in cultures with a greater collectivist and Power-Distance emphasis

(Hofstede). In my work in Singapore, I've noticed that young people studying in institutions that have adopted more Western styles of teaching are being exposed to debate and are encouraged to develop points of view. This can create tensions when they start work because their culture is traditionally more deferential. Whilst the research findings provide a useful guide, in cross-cultural situations the real value comes in having a dialogue around the data. What was the impact of a particular level of reacting behaviour in a specific cross-cultural context?

For most of us, Supporting and Disagreeing are everyday behaviours and facts of life. If they are not being articulated you can be certain that they're being thought, especially so in the case of Disagreeing. At some point, what you're thinking will be given away in what you say and do, so it's better to develop a more skilful way of handling these two behaviours. More than that, Supporting and Disagreeing are powerful allies in building a positive and constructive climate at work. When you use Supporting, people know you've noticed their contributions and that recognition in turn tends to create a degree of loyalty. Constructive, skilful Disagreeing is an important life skill. Conflict will inevitably occur. It's how we handle it that matters.

In responding to other people try this three-step process for handling your reactions:

1 **Take the time to listen to what they say**

2 **Then ask questions to evaluate, and**

3 **Then react.**

```
┌─────────────────────────────────────────┐
│   Take the time to listen to what they say │
└─────────────────────────────────────────┘
                    ↓
┌─────────────────────────────────────────┐
│      Then ask questions to evaluate        │
└─────────────────────────────────────────┘
                    ↓
┌─────────────────────────────────────────┐
│              Then react                    │
└─────────────────────────────────────────┘
```

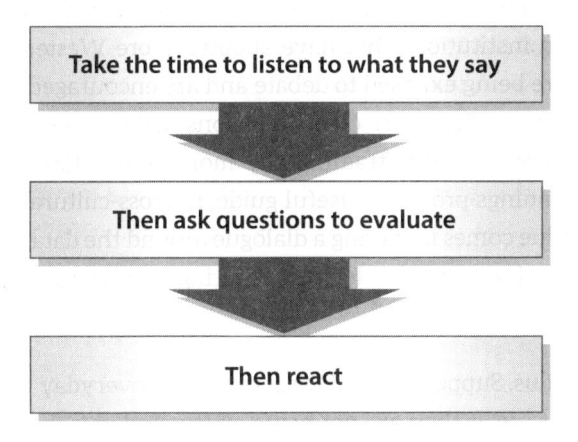

Fig 19. Managing Your Reactions

Supporting and Disagreeing are two of the three Reacting behaviours. The third is Defending-Attacking.

Defending-Attacking

Defending-Attacking is a behaviour where you 'attack' another person or you 'defend' yourself. Where Disagreeing is rational, Defending-Attacking is often laden with emotion and judgment.

You may remember reading earlier that no one behaviour category is either 'good' or 'bad'. It's about what's appropriate in a given situation. Defending-Attacking can be used humorously in some cultures: in the UK we call it 'banter', while in France the word for it is 'badinage'. Sometimes, however, banter can be alienating.

> Kurnia was a new member of a well-established team working in a manufacturing business. He had joined the UK team from his native Indonesia. Talking about his first few weeks, he described them as "difficult" and told of feeling "cut off" from the rest of the team. Kurnia felt uncomfortable in the team because it was normal

for the guys to bandy around insults. Kurnia thought the behaviour was rude and he also felt excluded because he didn't understand the back-story to the offensive, but apparently jokey, exchanges.

In this instance, the existing UK team saw their use of Defending-Attacking behaviour as harmless fun. They were experiencing that pleasure-induced dopamine hit. For Kurnia, however, it was both unpleasant and unwelcoming. In his native Indonesia this sort of behaviour is seen as insulting. Kurnia felt ignored and offended and his brain processed his social pain as physical pain.

There are times when Defending-Attacking can be both powerful and effective. Recently I sat in on a meeting where two participants were over-excited and not focussing on the subjects under discussion. After some time (and some considerable disruption) one of the team said: "Oh for heaven's sake you two, isn't it time you started acting your age?" It caused the belligerent pair to settle down and focus on the contribution that was required of them – an example of where Defending-Attacking can be useful.

Defending-Attacking is almost always a low-scoring behaviour. It occurs less or not at all in some cultures, most notably Asian ones. Regardless of culture, when Defending-Attacking behaviour does arise it's worth exploring the impact. Sometimes Defending-Attacking is perceived as being downright rude. Other times it may be used as a way of establishing your status, even if this runs the risk of humiliating others.

High Defending-Attacking is symptomatic of relationships that have reached breaking point. The attack or defence means the issue under discussion has been overtaken by personalised comments. Repeated use of the Defending-Attacking behaviour creates a downward spiral of mood and climate and an upward spiral of tension, frequently resulting in a crisis. This kind of situation is best avoided. When in doubt, stick with the issue and use Disagreeing. If your emotions are taking hold, then opt for Giving Feelings to articulate what's going on for you at that moment in time, rather than attack the other person.

Defending-Attacking or Giving Feelings: which is preferable?

D-A *"You're just being bloody ridiculous!"*

GF *"I'm uncomfortable with that idea."*

D-A *"That's so typical of you accountants, always using the numbers to deceive!"*

GF *"I'm anxious about the level of transparency."*

Developing skilful use of Reacting behaviours will create greater transparency and help you to build working relationships. Understanding how to facilitate reactions in others will again help with transparency and create a more positive work environment.

Summary of key points

- The three Reacting behaviours are: Supporting, Disagreeing and Defending-Attacking

- In group/team interactions, research suggests that Supporting and Disagreeing behaviours should account for 10-20% of the behavioural budget and be in balance

- A Low Reactor is someone who spends less than 10% on Supporting and Disagreeing. This can be problematic because people don't know where you're coming from. Try increasing Supporting behaviour

- High Disagreeing, and in particular Labelled Disagreeing, can lead to you being perceived as 'negative' and 'obstructive'. Alternative behaviours include: Building, Testing Understanding and Giving Feelings

- High Supporting and Low Disagreeing tends to occur where popularity prevails over prudence. Explore why this is happening

- A High Reactor is an individual who spends more than 20% on Supporting and Disagreeing. Ask them questions to test their thinking and slow them down. Watch for other signs of stress

- Not all Reacting behaviours travel cross-culturally

- Beware the Defending-Attacking spiral. Try to stick with the issue and use Disagreeing or Giving Feelings as alternatives

CHAPTER 7
Expressing Feelings

"Happiness in intelligent people is the rarest thing I know."

Ernest Hemingway

Your emotions influence much more than you might imagine: for example, how you build relationships, handle conflict, manage stress, and create a productive work environment. As well as being conveyed through our body language and facial expressions, emotions play a role in influencing our behaviour, as evidenced through work by researchers such as Wood Brooks, Barsade and O'Neill.

Why is it helpful to express feelings?

By 'expressing feelings' I don't mean unleashing a tidal wave of emotion. Rather I'm talking about intermittent references to how you are feeling in relation to the work you're doing. At work, interactions happen all the time, and how you're feeling forms part of what you bring to those interactions. You're giving a commentary of your feelings at a point in time: for example: "I feel energised, concerned, frustrated, happy..." Articulating those feelings can have a very positive impact on the mood of any interaction, as we'll see later.

A major influencer in the success of teams is the level of social distance between team members (Neeley). Broadly speaking, the better the team members connect emotionally, the better the performance of the team. Teams where disharmony exists risk getting sidetracked by their interpersonal issues. Expressing your feelings can contribute to the emotional connection within a team and reduce the social distance. In their pursuit of the 'perfect team', Google found that high-performing teams all had high 'average social sensitivity', which includes expressing and intuiting feelings.

For many of us these feelings sit below the surface, particularly the negative emotions. As illustrated in the 'Cultural Iceberg' model, what we see above the waterline is the behaviour in the interaction. What sits below it are the beliefs, values and feelings that are often subconscious. But the feelings sometimes bubble up. You may think you've submerged them but they find a way to influence your behaviour, often in inappropriate ways.

CHAPTER 7

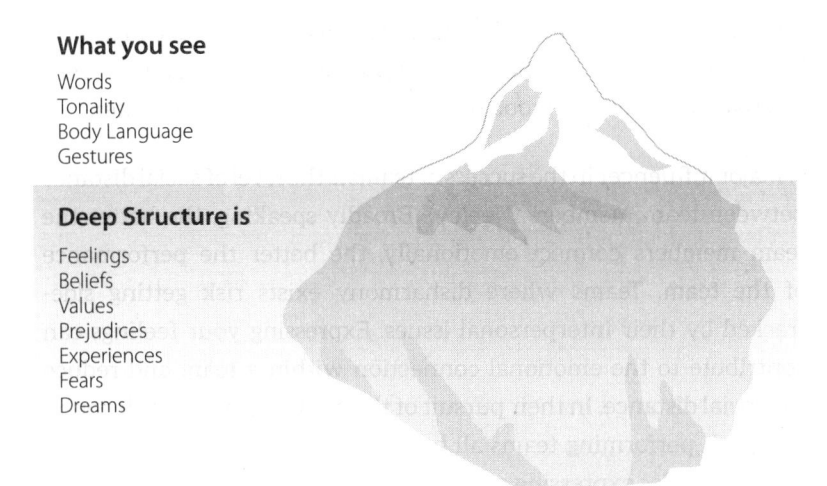

What you see
Words
Tonality
Body Language
Gestures

Deep Structure is
Feelings
Beliefs
Values
Prejudices
Experiences
Fears
Dreams

Adapted from *Beyond Culture* - Edward T. Hall

Fig 20. The Cultural Iceberg

Tomas was presenting some recommendations for recruitment to his fellow board members. During his presentation he'd been interrupted a number of times and it was clear to me that he was feeling frustrated. He wanted to complete his presentation but the repeated questioning was throwing him off-track. Then, as if from out of nowhere, Tomas protested: "Do you want me to finish or don't you? I'm trying to talk you through my proposals and all you can do is interrupt me. I'm sick to death of it." His colleagues were shocked. They hadn't seen this coming. Tomas's emotions had triumphed but he had left his fellow board members bemused.

Unexpressed emotions can be overwhelming. They can also leave you feeling exhausted because of the energy required to contain them. Sometimes the desire to disconnect from what you're feeling can be so strong that you seem cut off from what is happening.

Why can we find it difficult to express emotions readily or skilfully?

I've had the occasion to witness emotional outbursts many times in my career. Often such outbursts leave the unsuspecting victims feeling threatened or alienated. I've also experienced skilful, successful people being simply overwhelmed by the burden of emotional baggage they are carrying, so much so that their otherwise constructive contributions are rendered almost inaudible through tears.

Some organisational cultures inhibit the expression of emotional language, resulting in a lack of positive role modelling in emotional expression. An argument I hear for keeping emotions under wraps (more often from guys than from women) is that "it's a sign of weakness". At which point my heart sinks. (See Tannen's work on how linguistics influence behaviour at work.)

In the previous chapter we explored the three Reacting behaviours and their impact. Here we'll look at two other behaviours that can help you to express more of your feelings: *Giving Feelings* and *Open behaviour*. Both these behaviours originate from Rackham and Carlisle's studies on effective negotiators, and over many years of observing interactions we've found them also to have a positive impact in team and group work and two-way discussions.

Giving Feelings

Definition: Giving Feelings involves an expression of one's feeling about the current situation, as in:

> "I'm uncomfortable that we haven't explored all the possibilities."

> "I'm excited about the progress we're making."

Open Behaviour

Definition: Open behaviour is the non-defensive admission of mistakes or shortcomings.

> "I'm sorry, maybe I haven't thought it through well enough."

> "That's probably my fault. I was making an informed guess."

Giving Feelings

This behavioural concept originates from research into effective negotiators who were found to use such behaviour to express both positive and negative emotions about how the negotiations were progressing.

I saw a similar process in my work with banks and insurance companies. Later, I used the same behaviour when, as a business development consultant, I had to negotiate long-term commercial arrangements with clients. As I began to do more and more observations of group work and multi-stakeholder interactions, I saw similarities between the profiles of successful negotiators and those of successful group leaders and members. One such similarity was the use of Giving Feelings.

> *One client in particular, a man called Joseph, used this behaviour with people from very different disciplines and businesses: engineers, bosses, HR, Health and Safety Executive, community action groups, politicians, and trades union representatives. For example, in a community meeting focussing on the decommissioning of a power plant (with all the attendant risks), Joseph addressed the anxious audience thus: "I know this is difficult for everyone but I'm really encouraged by the quality of discussion we're having here today."*

> All Joseph's colleagues without exception described him in positive terms, using words such as 'skilful', 'approachable', 'human' and 'warm'. And yet some of the discussions Joseph engaged in were tough, challenging and tense. It was very powerful that he was described so favourably even when he was driving a hard bargain or adopting an unpopular position.

In interactions generally it can be helpful to voice how you're feeling about the way the work is progressing, be that the task aspect or the dynamics of the group. Such expression, which can include both positive and negative feelings, helps those involved gauge their progress. This can be particularly useful when working in a multi-national group where fluency in the company's adopted language can vary significantly.

Emotions are contagious, so if you bring expressions of positive affect to your interactions it's likely other people will catch the bug. Furthermore, there's an ever-growing body of research linking the expression of feelings to establishing and increasing trust in relationships (for example, Jarvenpaa and Leidner, Hakanen and Soudunsari).

Describing one's emotion activates the ventromedial prefrontal cortex in the brain, which down-regulates the amygdala's more forceful responses, controlling the intensity of the emotional reaction. As the saying goes: "Name it, claim it, tame it, aim it." If we can give voice to our emotions, we can accept them and, where necessary, overcome them and then decide what to do with them.

> Tsung Wei was working with a group of his peers on an innovation challenge. This was the first time the group of six had worked together. They came from different disciplines and different countries. They had just four hours to tackle the challenge and prepare to present to the Chief Innovation Officer. Throughout this time I observed the group at work. Tsung Wei used Giving Feelings

to reflect his positive perspective on how the team was doing. For example:

"I'm really pleased with the progress we're making."

"This is really exciting."

"I'm getting nervous but I think we're in good shape."

The group felt encouraged by Tsung Wei's feelings. They reported an increase in confidence about what they were working on and how they were working together.

Louise, a manager in a project team, was trying to work with her team in a way that encouraged them to take initiative and responsibility, regardless of grade and job title. In one meeting the team kept reverting to Louise for all the decision-making. After some time Louise said: "I just want you to know that I am feeling really uncomfortable. I'm noticing that when it comes to making decisions everyone looks to me." This was enough to help the team start to explore why this was so. On this basis they were able to discuss what needed to be in place to foster greater autonomy.

Creating an opportunity to capture feelings allows the group to take stock. How comfortable is everyone feeling? What's the degree of clarity in the group? What's working (or not)? The Exit Surveys referenced in Chapter 3 can be used to assess the emotional mood of the team. In that chapter you also read about 'The Round'. You can use this technique to test the pulse of the group, inviting each person in turn to express an emotion or one word that describes how he or she is feeling. Listening attentively to what people say about their emotions is vital, and it can be helpful to ask questions for clarification. As Stephen Covey says: "Seek first to understand rather than be understood."

Open behaviour

In his seminal work *Good to Great*, Jim Collins describes the factors that differentiate great companies from merely good ones. One of these factors is 'Level 5 Leadership', where the leaders of great companies are described as having a 'paradoxical blend of personal humility and professional will'. The humility is characterised as mild-mannered, self-effacing and understated. These leaders look to give credit where credit is due, rather than claim it for themselves. When it comes to errors or mistakes, they take responsibility rather than apportion blame elsewhere.

'Open' is the behaviour that best demonstrates this humility. And, like Collins, we've found its use to be a differentiator between average and skilful performers. Open behaviour is given to admitting mistakes ("I'm sorry I messed up there") and revealing shortcomings ("I have to confess I didn't really understand it"). Far from being a sign of weakness, Open behaviour reveals a lack of vanity and a willingness to take personal responsibility for the issue or inadequacy. If you're in a more junior position, using Open behaviour can create an opportunity for learning and demonstrating improvement. When used by a manager or leader, it can be a helpful leveller. Admitting you've got something wrong reveals fallibility and helps you appear more human. More often than not, your fallibility will cause people to respond positively rather than critically. Where fault is not acknowledged by the 'offender', this typically frustrates others in the interaction.

However, offering an apology or admitting fallibility may not always be appropriate or helpful. Cultural contexts vary. For example, in Japan the use of Open behaviour "I'm sorry" is more typically an acknowledgement of the other person's discomfort. And research by Tannen suggests that women's greater likelihood to admit being at fault can result in the overuse of apology, which can backfire on them.

In general, however, not getting something right is an opportunity for learning. Open behaviour is the first step in that process and a necessary behaviour for building resilience: the ability to *"remain adaptive under strain"* (Pemberton).

> *Alex was a new manager. He was keen to involve his team in a new training programme he was delivering and invited one of the team, Sacha, to take the lead on day 1 of an event. Sacha did not do a good job. Her delivery was ill-prepared and lacked confidence. Alex's response was to tell her: "I'm sorry for putting you in that position. I now realise I didn't do enough to check what you were planning and I didn't help to prepare you adequately. That was my mistake."*

Think of a recent situation where, like Alex, you got something wrong. Perhaps it was a performance discussion that was clumsily handled. Maybe you gave a customer some incorrect information. Or were you guilty of putting someone forward for a task for which they were ill-prepared? How could you have used Open behaviour? What would that sound like? Make a note of what you might say in the space below:

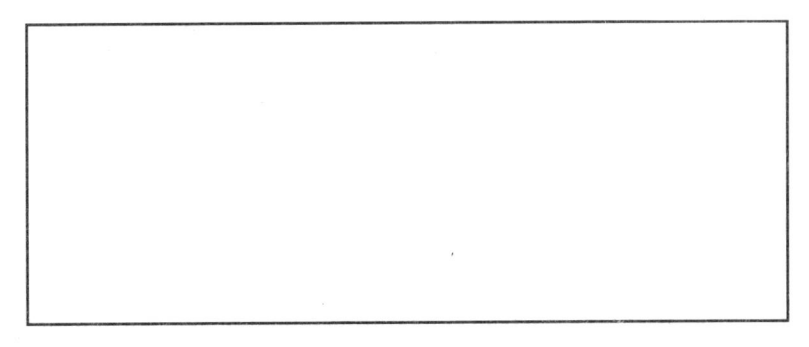

Perhaps you work in an organisation where there are good role models for these behaviours and you've witnessed first-hand the power of their contributions. If you have no role models, now is your opportunity. As Gandhi said: "Be the change you want to see in the world."

Summary of key points

- The better that team members connect emotionally, the better they perform

- Ignoring feelings can create stress

- Lack of expression of feelings may cause you to appear unfriendly or arrogant

- Giving Feelings is a constructive way to comment on how you feel about the work you're engaged in – either the task itself and/or the process of working together

- Open behaviour is consistent with Level 5 Leadership and demonstrates humility and is essential for resilience

CHAPTER 8
Influencing Others

> "Know the difference between impressing people and influencing them. Impressing them changes what they think. Influencing them changes what they do."
>
> Anon.

The Cambridge dictionary defines the verb 'to influence' thus:

> "To affect or change how someone or something develops, behaves or thinks."

When influencing others you're trying to get agreement or buy-in from another (or others) in order to help them move from their current position to a new and different one. The opportunities and demands for influence at work are huge. You have to influence your staff and others where you don't have authority. You also need to influence upwards. It follows that the skill of influencing is critical in business. When was the last time you tried to influence someone at work? How successful were you?

In a conversation with Rachel, a manager in a professional services firm, we identified 11 opportunities for persuasion over the next 48 hours of her work. Among these were:

- Kicking off a new project with her team
- Having performance appraisal conversations
- Writing a proposal
- Having a client meeting
- Reviewing the agenda for a community of practice
- Convincing her boss to promote a team member

In each of these situations Rachel was trying to do one of two things. She either wanted to convince someone of an idea that she was already committed to, or she wanted to explore ideas with another person or people and reach a decision. In both instances it was her belief that she was trying to reach the best solution, be that hers or somebody else's.

A variety of studies have highlighted the number of influencing styles in operation at work, with some identifying as many as nine different styles (Falbe and Yukl). Most of us have a default style, one we feel most comfortable using. To be effective in our influencing, we need to be able to select the most appropriate style and therefore the most appropriate behaviours.

In this chapter we'll focus on two particular influencing styles which Rackham calls 'Push' and 'Pull'. Subsequent work by Harrison and Berlew as they developed their *Positive Power & Influence Program* refers to the styles as 'Assertive Persuasion' and 'Participation and Trust', later developed further by Harrison and Kouzes. Push and Pull are respectively the most frequently used influencing styles, and the most successful in terms of gaining commitment.

Push-style influence

Push is the most commonly used influencing style. It's the default style for most people who have been through a logic-based education system.

The Push style of influencing goes like this:

- I have an idea or opinion that I'm committed to
- I share that with you
- I tell you the reasons why it's a good idea or why I believe I'm correct
- (Hopefully) you agree and move your position

Nicky, an R&D project manager, had a direct report who was repeatedly missing her delivery deadlines. She was disorganised and failed to track the progress of her various projects. Nicky used a Push style of influencing to suggest a way forward:

"I'd like you to complete a project management programme because you'll learn how to monitor and manage the progress of your projects. You'll also learn how to display your progress visually. Understanding this will help you to better integrate your work with the team, so that you can support each other through peaks and troughs."

In this example Nicky knew where she wanted her team member to move to. She generated the idea and gave her supporting reasons.

In a Push style the behaviours used are Proposing Content, Giving Information and Shutting Out. The solution comes from the influencer and it's the influencer who does most of the talking. We use this style day in and day out. But research by Falbe and Yukl suggests it is only effective 53% of the time. That's a 1 in 2 hit rate.

Rackham's research shows that Push works in conditions where the influencer has positional authority or expertise and where decisions need to be made very quickly. For example, when working with emergency response teams at Heathrow airport, he found that the most effective team leaders were 'Pushers'.

One of the weaknesses of employing a Push strategy is that you underestimate the amount of resistance you may encounter. And because you reveal your solution early on in a Push strategy you may be doomed almost before you've started. Damage caused by an ineffective use of Push can take a long time to repair.

I remember a group of friends taking me to London for the day on my birthday. We thought it would be great to get some late availability tickets for a show. The conversation went like this:

Jenny: Let's go and see *The Forbidden Planet*.

Ally: That's not really my thing

Paul: No, you'll love it. The music's great!

Ally: It's Fifties music, isn't it?

Jenny: Yes, so cool. And it's a great cast.

Ally: If I'm truthful it wouldn't be my first choice.

Jenny: But really, it'll be so much fun!

In the end I capitulated. I thought it was better to have my friendships endure than ungraciously stamp my feet in rejection of their generosity. (And yes, Reader, I hated it!)

Sometimes, like me, you'll give in to the force of the argument. On other occasions you may find yourself less compliant. You push back with Disagreeing or compete by Proposing (alternative) Content or, more skilfully, with a question.

Resistance to Push

If you've been the one using a Push style, try to recall situations where you have used Push for what you thought was a clear logical position, only to find that your rationale was apparently ignored.

> *Craig had been instructed by his boss (who used a Push style) to complete a safety investigation report within a two-week timeframe. When the due date arrived the report was nowhere to be seen. The email exchange was evidence that the message the boss had sent was indeed the message Craig had received. And yet he hadn't met the deadline. Following discussions with his boss, it transpired that Craig didn't agree with his boss's view of the incident and was reluctant to fall in line.*

In this situation, Craig's boss was convinced by his solution and had instructed Craig on that basis. Craig's inability to deliver was driven by his resistance. You can doubtless recall similar situations where a clearly articulated Push style has not had the desired traction. It's all a matter of resistance.

Whenever you find yourself wanting to influence another person, it's useful to begin by spending some time thinking about the potential 'reasons to resist'. What reasons or factors, whether logical or emotional, might lead the person to stand fast in their current position and not be swayed into moving?

Imagine a situation where I am responsible for implementing a new back office system to support you in your daily work. I come to talk to you about the rollout. What might be your reasons to resist? Take three minutes to jot them down in the space provided below (time yourself and stop when the three minutes are up).

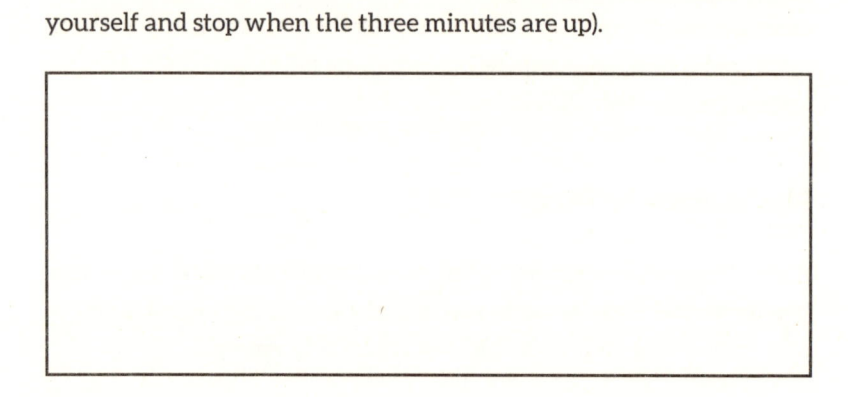

I did a similar exercise recently in an organisation where this was about to happen. I asked the team I was working with to take three minutes to list their reasons to resist. One group member generated 31 reasons: an incredible rate of one reason every six seconds (or 5.81 seconds to be precise). Perhaps that was an indication of just how deep her seam of resistance lay. The value of the exercise was in helping the system 'owner' understand what he was up against. Forewarned is forearmed. The greater the number of reasons, the harder his influencing task. Understanding the Behaviour Analysis of resistance helped him to identify those issues he could mitigate and where there might be more challenge.

Of course you don't always have the luxury of time to consider reasons to resist at length. But you can probably make an informed guess at the overall level of resistance you're likely to face – and the extent to which it matters. We'll return to this point later when exploring the key factors influencing your choice of style.

Pull style

Pull is the most successful of the influencing styles, registering a mere 18% on the resistance scale. It goes like this:

- I ask you for your ideas

- You offer some options

- I ask questions to explore your suggestions

- I build on your suggestions

- We agree on a way forward

In exercising a Pull style you'll be using three behaviours in particular: Seeking Proposals, Seeking Information, and Building. While a Pull style isn't pure Seeking, it predominantly uses questions to generate an outcome *together* with the other person.

Pull style is appropriate when helping people to think and reflect on situations and behaviours. I've seen it having a hugely positive impact in performance conversations. Instead of the manager pronouncing on an employee's performance, he/she makes use of a series of questions to help the individual critically evaluate their performance and determine their on-going development goals.

Pull is also very powerful in generating commitment. This is because those using it are genuinely interested in the ideas someone else puts forward. It's also a useful style to use with a team because it allows you to explore multiple ideas together.

The risk with an authentic Pull style is that the other person's thoughts are outside your control, so you have no idea where you may end up. If you're a control freak, this style will be a challenge for you to employ.

Sometimes you may start a conversation using a Pull style, hoping to draw on the resourcefulness of the other people. Where they are limited in their ability to respond you may need to resort to Push or to frame a solution in the form of a question, for example:

What if you did X?

Do you think it might be helpful to try… … …?

I often see Pull style used badly. This can be for one of two reasons:

1. The influencer's questioning skill is limited
2. The influencer has a hidden agenda

Both of these situations are repairable.

Ask more questions

I often tell my clients: "If you take just one thing away from this workshop it would be this: give less, ask more, ask better." This is because most people spend too much time offering their own thoughts, ideas and opinions and insufficient time attending to the views of others. However, if you're trying to use a Pull style you're heading in the right direction because you're asking more questions. The next step is to ask more varied questions:

Fig 21. Asking More Varied Questions

You can ask for reasons:

> "What leads you to think this will work?"

> "Why do you say that?"

You can also seek reactions:

> "What do you think?"

> "How does that feel?"

Here's how my friends might have used Pull style in the birthday treat situation sketched earlier:

Jenny: What kinds of shows do you prefer?

Ally: It depends. I like drama and comedy. Some musicals are OK but they wouldn't be my first choice.

Paul: Is there something you have in mind?

Ally: No, nothing in particular.

Jenny: Would you rather just go out for dinner?

Ally: No, I'd like to see a show.

Jenny: Let's take a look at what's on at the National. And should we plan to eat before or after?

Ally: I think after would be more relaxing.

Paul: What type of cuisine?

Ally: I really don't mind. There are lots of options close by – Thai, Lebanese...

Paul: Great. So let's check out the National and book a table somewhere on the South Bank. How does that sound?

Ally: Marvellous. Aren't I the lucky one!

Pull style is tricky to use because it's difficult to do well. It also takes longer. It requires more skilful questioning and it also requires you to let go of some control. This is because in an authentic use of Pull the person being influenced generates the solution. As you develop greater behavioural skill you can use Testing Understanding, Seeking Information, Building, Supporting and Disagreeing to shape the path to that solution. But it's *their* solution, not *yours*.

To help you focus on questions, try to remember this phrase: *"Be curious rather than judgmental"*. Being open to possibilities the other person generates can enhance the potential for learning. In the process, it can strengthen your relationship and generate a better quality outcome.

Hidden agendas

Influencers sometimes opt for a Pull style to encourage another person towards their pre-conceived view. This is a high-risk strategy because, once again, the other person's responses are outside your control. If they comply, you get what you wanted. But if they choose a different path, what then?

I had a boss once who was hell-bent on using a Pull style. He would always start a discussion with some open questions. When the course of the conversation went somewhere he wasn't anticipating he would then jump styles. Here's a very simple example to illustrate his ambiguous influencing technique:

Boss: We need to move the business development team to another location because of the building work. What are your

	thoughts?
Me:	Hmmm, I guess there are a number of options. We could move up onto the second floor or we could base ourselves in London for a while.
Boss:	What about using the meeting room? Had you thought of that?
Me:	No, I hadn't. I suppose it's a possibility but it'll be a bit tight. And how will we accommodate our internal meetings and client pitches?
Boss:	I'm sure we can find a way to cope.
Me:	What about the interview day? Where will we hold that?
Boss:	I think the meeting room is the best option. Thanks for your views. Let's move the team in tomorrow.

What was clear to me was that my boss had already decided on the meeting room as the temporary home for my team. So why didn't he just come clean? Where Pull style is used with a hidden agenda there's a high risk of the other person feeling manipulated. This is referred to by one of my colleagues as 'bogus consultation'. Rackham labelled this 'Partial Puller' and the research revealed it to be ineffective. My boss had no real interest in my views, so his use of Pull style was both inauthentic and unskilled.

Push or Pull: when to use each style

Four questions can help guide your choice of influencing style:

1. *Who has the power?*

2. *What's the level of resistance?*

3. *How many options are there?*

4. *How important is it to have the other person's commitment?*

Who has the power?

Where you have the power, be that positional or through expertise, it's appropriate to use a Push style. However, using your authority (positional power) may result in compliance or resistance rather than commitment: in other words, a Win : Lose outcome. Overuse of positional power to give credence to a Push style is likely to lose you a lot of friends and win you a few enemies, so this is a tactic to be used sparingly. As a former boss once sagely advised: "Choose your battles wisely."

If you want to have a long-term, value-adding relationship with a client or colleague, the focus must be on the relationship. How can you best help them while avoiding an "I know better than you" position?

Where you have expertise and the other person lacks knowledge (for example, someone new to the organisation or new to a position), then a Push style is both legitimate and helpful.

When both you and the other person have expertise, this creates a very different dynamic. It's all too easy for two experts to adopt different positions and never reach agreement, driving up the scores of Disagreeing and Giving Information. Instead of getting into a tit-for-tat round of "my idea's better than yours", try to agree what you both want to achieve (Seeking Proposals and Seeking Information) and then co-create the best way of getting there.

What's the level of resistance?

The greater the resistance the more likely you'll need to use a Pull style. Here the aim is to understand the other person's position. Only then can you identify common ground and collaborate to find a mutually acceptable solution.

However, there will be some circumstances where you'll choose to use a Push style in spite of the resistance. Sometimes you'll need to push ahead with a solution without consultation. If goodwill exists in the relationship you can probably afford to use a Push style with little or no consequence. But if you push ahead in situations where you haven't established goodwill you may damage the relationship. Therefore, when selecting your influencing style, it's important to consider the likely impact.

How many options are there?

In certain situations there are no options: there's only one solution. For example, I work a lot in the petrochemical industry where Health and Safety regulations leave no room for ambiguity. For many processes there is just one way, one solution.

The best way to illustrate this is to invite you to think of us sitting in a meeting room. The fire alarm sounds. At that point I will inform you of the fire procedure and how to get to the muster point. In such situations only a Push style will do. It would be foolhardy for me to employ a Pull style, as in:

> *"Oh, that's the fire alarm. What should we do?"*

Instead, using a Push style, I'd say something like:

> *"That's the fire alarm. You need to leave your belongings here and follow me to the muster point, which is just over in the car park."*

However, in circumstances where numerous possible options abound a Pull style will work best. As the saying goes: "There's more than one way to skin a cat." For example, imagine a team meeting where we are discussing the Christmas party:

Me: What should we do for the Christmas party? (Seeking Proposals)

Pete: Is it with partners or not? (Seeking Information)

Me: What would you prefer? (Seeking proposals)

Carol: Without partners. (Proposing Content)

Pete: We could do some activity together and then head out for a meal. (Proposing Content)

Carol: We could make the meal the activity and then eat it together as a means of celebration. (Building)

Nick: Then we could go out dancing. (Building)

Simon: Or to a Karaoke bar. (Proposing content)

In short, where there's choice, select Pull. Where there's only one way, select Push.

How important is commitment?

In your influencing task, to what extent do you need and want people to be committed to the solution? If you require a high level of commitment, your strategy should involve others as much as possible in determining the solution. And this points to using a Pull style. The level of commitment you can achieve through involving people is not to be underestimated. It's often worth going for what you might consider a sub-optimal solution as a trade-off for that increased commitment. It's a stepping-stone. You're gaining engagement, trust and motivation as a trade-off for control and perfection (which after all rarely exists).

If you stop to consider the issues of power, resistance, options and commitment involved in your influencing task, this will help you select the style most appropriate for the situation, maximising your chances of success. You need to be able to use both styles, and use them well. Letting go of control when using a Pull style may feel uncomfortable at first, so choose situations where you have little to lose and slowly build your confidence.

It's not about 'tone'

Push and Pull styles of influencing have nothing to do with tone.

You can Push in a gentle way and you can Pull in an aggressive way. What differentiates each style is the dominant behaviours involved:

Push: High on *Proposing Content, Giving Information and Shutting Out*

Pull: High on *Seeking Proposals, Testing Understanding and Building*

A final point – The likeability factor

The degree to which you like someone will affect your openness to his or her influence. Can you imagine a tyrant advertising children's cereal? How well you influence will be swayed by your likeability factor. Likeability increases with (positive) familiarity and by the level of trust that exists between you and others. It's about what happens at what my colleague Hilary Lines calls the 'Touchpoint' of your relationship with another person. Behaviourally this means developing a flexible behavioural repertoire across the 15 categories so that you can expertly use each of them as the situation demands.

Summary of key points

- Influencing is a key skill for effective performers

- Push style is high on Proposing Content and Giving Information. The solution is revealed early on and can be met with resistance. Push style meets with resistance – both overt and covert – 47% of the time

- Push works best when:

    - You have the power and/or the knowledge

    - There's only one way

    - Resistance is low or of no consequence

    - It's an urgent matter or time is short

    - The decision has already been taken

    - You can enforce compliance

- It's useful to consider the other person's potential reasons to resist when considering your influencing strategy

- Pull style is more difficult to use but meets with less resistance – just 18%. It's high on Seeking Proposals, Testing Understanding and Building

- Avoid phoney Pull where you already have a solution in mind, otherwise you may be perceived as manipulative

- Give less, ask more, then ask better questions to perfect the Pull style

- Pull works best when:

- The persuader accepts they are inexpert

- You don't have the power

- There's more than one solution

- Resistance is high

- There are no time pressures

- Any movement is better than none

- You want to coach/develop someone to use their resources

- You want to foster a sense of partnership or collaboration

- Consider your 'likeability' factor and which behaviours might enhance it

CHAPTER 9
Behaviour Analysis in Virtual Teams

Virtual teams and telecommuting are now well-established features of corporate life and continue to be on the rise. Branded by Haas and Mortensen as '4D teams', virtual collaborators are 'diverse, dispersed, digital and dynamic'. Aided by technology you can connect with team members almost any time, anywhere. You can join a meeting from your downtown office as easily as you can conduct an appraisal conversation from your kitchen table.

Engaging with people in real time across geographic boundaries, be they national, international or global, works best when you can see and hear the other people as if they were in the same room. Many of these ethernet exchanges are also supported by tools that allow data-sharing and online Q&A. And what were once considered barriers to communication – multiple languages, different time zones, erratic technologies, interference and interruptions – are now embraced as the norm.

What you have been reading about Behaviour Analysis is just as relevant in this virtual environment. Indeed, many of the lessons from Behaviour Analysis are best emphasised if you are striving to make a difference in your long-distance discussions.

> Nadia was managing a project team from her base in Prague. Other team members were in Canada, Brazil and Thailand. They had weekly conference calls that varied in length and attendance. In reviewing the project, Nadia expressed her frustration that the team members said very little on the conference calls and that they weren't making progress quickly enough. Using a checklist for managing global meetings, Nadia was able to identify what behaviours to use to increase involvement, engagement and productivity. Within a month the team performance had improved through 100% attendance and catching up on the milestones that had slipped.

Here is the checklist I used with Nadia. It comprises ten considerations for driving up performance in a virtual team, together with the behaviours that will support you. You can act on each of these considerations regardless of your position in the team. Use your behavioural skill to help your colleagues be the best 4D team possible.

1. Establish clear rules for working together

Clear rules help you get the work done more efficiently and effectively. At the outset it's useful to explore and agree how often you'll connect, and for how long. Also, what happens in the space between diarised interactions? Establishing this clarity provides a drumbeat for your interactions which is overlaid by the percussion of appropriate ground rules: for example, everyone will arrive online on time; don't interrupt the speaker. These are particularly helpful where people have different cultural expectations about what is acceptable.

In setting the tone of the working relationships you'll need to decide how much you Push or Pull the norms. Are you seeking collaboration and inclusion or command and control? And what might be the consequences?

In opting for a collaborative approach the behavioural sequence may flow something like this:

Proposing procedure: "I thought it might be useful to spend a few minutes agreeing how we should work together."

Seeking proposals: "How often do you think we should connect in these early stages?"

Proposing content: "What about once a week?"

Building: "And we could make that Monday."

The key behaviours are the Initiating behaviours: Proposing Procedure, Proposing Content, Building and Seeking Proposals. The intent is to gather input from all the team members, increasing their commitment to the process and the outcomes. Also, let's remember the importance of Summarising to confirm what has been discussed and agreed.

As new members join the team it is worth re-visiting and re-evaluating the group norms. Are they effective? What more do you need to do to improve your ways of working?

2. Create a shared direction

A common sense of purpose and agreed outcomes are particularly important for a remote team where it's all too easy for people to go off-track. It is helpful to define both what the direction is and what this means for each person involved.

Again, your influencing strategy will determine the behaviours you use. Is it appropriate for you to impose a direction and opt for a Push style? Perhaps the destination has been decided but you can involve others in influencing how you reach it by using a Pull style. Or maybe you have a blank canvas, another opportunity to exercise those Pull muscles.

3. Build trust and familiarity

This is much harder to achieve when you are in one location while your colleagues are scattered across five other countries. High performing teams treat trust-building as a priority, and with good reason. As human beings we are pack animals with an innate need to belong. To help you and your colleagues feel you are of the same tribe, or at least share some common ground, you can create some social time in your meetings, inviting people to share something of their personal and professional self. And, believe it or not, it's the personal details that resonate most.

Behaviourally, you can tell a story, share a fact, or recount what you did at the weekend: each instance leads you to Give Information. Open behaviour (an admission of an error, mistake or shortcoming) is likely to accelerate trust. Responding warmly to people's contributions using Supporting and Giving Feelings creates a sense of safety within the group.

4. Share the airtime

You've already read about the importance of shared airtime, including the findings of the Google study. Research by Jarvenpaa and Leidner on trust in global virtual teams found that high trust teams had 'predictable communication patterns'. By this they mean that the team members' contribution levels were spread more evenly.

This finding suggests a focus on quality of contribution rather than quantity.

In managing the distribution of airtime, each team member has a responsibility to keep track of who is in (or out of) the conversation and to rectify the balance through the use of Bringing In, most frequently paired with Seeking Proposals or Seeking Information:

> "Brian, what's your view on the amount of contingency we need in this phase of the project?"
>
> "Amy, what do you think of Brian's suggestion?"

Establishing predictable communication patterns also benefits from you consciously monitoring the level of your own contributions when compared with others. Are you taking too much of the airtime?

5. Share the lead

In their work on power and trust in global virtual teams, Panteli and Tucker found that the more successful teams shared leadership across team members, depending on where the relevant knowledge lay. This makes sense. In a well-managed project, each activity stream has a **'single point of accountability'** (SPOA), an individual who is responsible for that strand of work. Allowing each SPOA to lead on his/her stream nurtures that accountability and often provides a development opportunity for a team member. If you're a team leader, it's important to remember you don't have to hold all the cards in your hand: you can practice your skills of delegation.

Proposing Procedure is a helpful behaviour for a SPOA or topic leader to practice. You can explain what you're going to cover, how long it will take and what you need from the other team members. For example:

> *"I'm going to take you through the risk register. Because it's the first time you have seen this, I'll spend five minutes going through each of the risks to ensure we have a shared understanding, and then I'll dip into those risks with a 'red' rating. I'd like you to let me know if I've missed anything out."*

6. Allocate roles

Regarding the team roles we explored in Chapter 4 (Timekeeper, Minute-taker, Scribe, Bridger), a dispersed team can benefit from a Scribe, who is adept at using technology so that discussion points are captured for all to see, and a Knowledge Manager, who acts as the team curator.

Allocating roles across the team and rotating these roles is another mechanism for distributing leadership. Here's a reminder of the key behaviours for each role:

Timekeeper: Giving Information and Seeking Proposals

Minute-taker: Testing Understanding and Seeking Information

Scribe: Testing Understanding and Seeking Information

Bridger: Across the 15 categories

The Knowledge Manager is one role where Giving Information is likely to be more appropriate.

7. Exploit diversity

In a global team you'll most likely have cultural, professional and personal diversity. High performing teams know the make-up of their diversity and work hard to leverage the value from the differing perspectives. And where diversity doesn't exist (or more likely is less pronounced), they will create it.

Margerison and McCann's work has found that high performing teams cover eight different team roles that each comprise a combination of types of work (e.g. upholding standards or creating ideas) and personal preferences (e.g. working with details, or requiring constant stimulus to keep boredom at bay). Covering all eight roles often requires members of the team to work outside their preferences. Behaviourally this means finding ways to handle the unfamiliar or something at odds with your personal preferences.

In her excellent book *Quiet (The Power of Introverts in a World That Can't Stop Talking)* Susan Cain describes how introverts can behave like extroverts where they consider work to be important and meaningful. The pretence of being an extrovert is in the service of a job well done.

Working contrary to type means learning new behaviours and building different behavioural muscle, depending on the role you are fulfilling. Making the most of the diversity around you relies on your curiosity. Key behaviours are Seeking Proposals, Seeking Information and Testing Understanding.

8. Facilitate round-the-clock working

Many global virtual teams, particularly in the technology sector, relay work around the globe from one time zone to another. Behaviourally you can master the passing of the baton by providing a clear explanation of progress to date (Giving Information), suggesting or asking what needs to happen next (Proposing Content or Seeking Proposals), inviting and giving reactions (Seeking Information, Supporting and Disagreeing) and appreciating what has been achieved (Supporting and Giving Feelings).

9. Value people's contributions

While all of us crave a sense of belonging, we also want to be appreciated and enjoy that dopamine hit. Regardless of whether you're a team leader or a team member, you can notice what people have achieved, the effort they've made and the way in which they are contributing to the discussion through the use of Supporting, Giving Feelings and Building:

Supporting: *"That's a great idea, Rohit."*

Giving Feelings: *"I'm so happy with what you've just done..."*

Building: *"....yes, and we can help you by providing some of the background information."*

10. Team leaders facilitate in the meeting and guide outside the meeting

Do you remember, back in Chapter 3, reading about the tension between task and process that a Chair or meetings manager can experience? As a leader, if you're acting on the previous nine considerations, you'll find yourself comfortably in the process zone as your team take care of the task. Here the key behaviours are: Proposing Procedure, Seeking Information, Testing Understanding, Summarising, Shutting Out and Bringing In.

The larger your team, the more susceptible you are to fragmented, unclear communications. This inevitably has an impact on levels of engagement and the priority team members give to the work. You can create clarity through the use of Seeking Information, Testing Understanding and Summarising.

In between the drumbeat of virtual meetings, like the conductor of an orchestra, you can work with each team member to question, refine and develop their work. Wherever possible you can lead with questions, helping them to draw on their resources, extend their networks and learn from what has been achieved (or not). You can shape their performance through the skilful use of Building and by providing feedback through the use of Supporting and Disagreeing. And sometimes you may find you need to provide some guidance through a suggestion (Proposing Content) or Giving Information.

Using your time well between meetings helps team members continue to generate and evaluate ideas, respond to each other and plan for the next session so that everyone is prepared, no one feels under pressure and everyone can make a contribution.

Summary of key points

- Behaviour Analysis is relevant and powerful in the context of virtual interactions

- There are 10 considerations for 4D teams:

    1. Establish clear rules for ways of working

    2. Create a shared direction

    3. Build relationships

    4. Share the airtime

    5. Share the lead

    6. Allocate roles

    7. Exploit diversity

    8. Facilitate round-the-clock working

    9. Value people's contributions

    10. Facilitate inside and guide outside the meeting

- Select the appropriate influencing strategy – Push or Pull?

CHAPTER 10

Putting Behaviour Analysis into Practice

"The way we speak is who we are
and who we want to be."

Deborah Tannen

Let's start this final chapter with an exercise. It'll take no longer than a few minutes of your time but it ensures you get a quick return on the time you've invested in reading this book.

I'm inviting you to spend just three minutes writing down as many answers that you can think of to this question: **"How can Behaviour Analysis help me?"**

Write your answers in the box below.

Next, ask yourself another question:

"How would my work colleagues say that Behaviour Analysis could help me?"

Take a further two minutes to write your answers in the box below.

Thank you!

In answering these questions, you'll have identified a number of ideas about how you could benefit from embracing Behaviour Analysis in your work. You may want to share your list with friendly critics who can support and perhaps challenge your perspectives.

Now you have the opportunity to identify ways by which you can make your Behaviour Analysis learning really stick.

"Doing it embeds it"

When we learn anything new, floundering is an important part of the discovery process. But out of confusion comes clarity. As you start to apply Behaviour Analysis you'll create new neural pathways in your brain. And as you repeatedly use these new pathways your brain will no longer need to consciously process what you're doing because your other-than-conscious mind takes over. You'll shift from unconscious incompetence to conscious incompetence, then on to conscious competence and finally to unconscious competence.

The speed at which you move through these phases depends on many things, most notably your openness to learning, especially as you shift from conscious incompetence to conscious competence. Using Behaviour Analysis before you forget what you've been reading will help your brain take notice and save this new information. You'll get an immediate return on investment from the time you have spent reading. As you start to apply Behaviour Analysis in your work, taking a few moments to review how you're doing will also help with retention and speed you up the learning curve.

Where do you start?

You will have many different opportunities to experiment with Behaviour Analysis. And I emphasise the word 'experiment' because I want to encourage you to play with the different categories.

There are two ways in which you can develop your mastery of the behaviour categories:

1. *Self-improvement*
2. *Behaviour Analysis coaching*

The following section on Self Improvement provides you with options and tools for helping you to self-direct your learning and application of Behaviour Analysis. In the section on Coaching you can read two case studies which illustrate different ways Behaviour Analysis has been used.

1. Self-improvement

Setting yourself clear behavioural goals is a fantastic place to begin and is within the gift of each and every one of us. Your choice of where to start will be influenced by the available interactions and your self-assessment of your behavioural skill.

The interactions you're involved in will require varied behaviours. A skilful negotiation requires different skills to those required for a project steering meeting. A fair and balanced performance appraisal calibration meeting demands a different skill profile to a brainstorming session.

When selecting a behaviour there are no hard and fast rules, because each interaction is different. However, some behaviours are easier to practise than others. And some have wider application. The list below illustrates my view of the order of priority for building your skill in each of the behaviour categories.

I have based this list according to three criteria: research that has identified the behavioural profile of skilled performers in a range of situations; behaviours that are often lacking – and much needed – in interactions; and behaviours that are easiest to begin with.

CHAPTER 10

Order of priority

1. Seeking Information
2. Seeking Proposals
3. Support
4. Proposing Procedure
5. Testing Understanding
6. Summarising
7. Proposing Content
8. Bringing In
9. Disagreeing
10. Giving Feelings
11. Open
12. Building
13. Shutting Out
14. Behaviour Labelling (not strictly a behaviour category but a skill worth developing)
15. Defending-Attacking
16. Giving Information

Here's some of the rationale for this order of priority.

Lead with questions

Questioning (and listening to the answer) is one of the most important behavioural skills. Socrates said: "Wonder is the beginning of wisdom." You help yourself and others to understand and learn and you show interest in other people's ideas. Remember the saying: "Give less, Ask more, Ask better."

Notice the positives

Listening to the discussions and identifying opportunities for supporting the contribution, idea or opinion can have a positive impact on the individual and the climate and can positively influence levels of trust.

Who manages the process?

Practising meetings management behaviours such as Proposing Procedure and Summarising will be easier if you are in the role of Chair or if no one else is doing this.

Be mindful of behaviours that don't always transfer culturally

The behaviours that disclose emotion and/or demonstrate humility do not transfer readily to all cultures. Defending-Attacking is unlikely to be helpful here, but improving how you articulate any disagreement may help increase your effectiveness – Testing Understanding, Disagreeing, Giving Feelings, Building.

Most people don't need to practise Giving Information

This is the category that almost always scores highest in people's behavioural budget, frequently over 50%. In fact, most of us would probably benefit from reducing our spend on Giving Information – by taking less airtime, avoiding repetition and practising being more succinct. Even if you're a low contributor seeking a greater share of the airtime, there are more skilful ways by which you can achieve your goal. To do something new you have to stop doing something you have done before. This makes it easier to focus on doing more of another behaviour category.

These factors must always be considered in the light of the context and your skill. If you're a lower contributor who wants to get in more, then Shutting Out may be a behavioural target. And remember, Shutting Out and Bringing In are always accompanied by another category. Which would you choose? If you frequently chair meetings, you might start by focussing on Proposing Procedure. You could then move on to Summarising, followed by Bringing In.

Start small

It's best to 'start small' by identifying low-risk situations and using differentiating behaviours such as Seeking Information. Set yourself a goal. For example:

> "In the next team meeting I will ask ten questions to encourage deeper exploration of the topics under discussion"

and later...

> "As ideas are generated I will reflect on them and then react"

and then...

"I will increase my level of support for both ideas and people"

Use the space below to think about a type of interaction you're regularly involved in – a meeting, a negotiation, a brainstorming session, a performance appraisal. Then identify your order of priority for developing your skills in that context. There's no need to create a list of 1 through 16: just focus on your top three. Now think about why you 'want to' focus on those three behaviours. Identifying why you 'want to' do something is more likely to result in a new behavioural habit forming than thinking in terms of 'I have to', which is likely to deplete your stores of willpower. Identify what actions you will take and by when. You may find it useful to share your goals with a colleague to increase your chances of acting as per your intent.

BEHAVIOUR	WHY I WANT TO GET BETTER	ACTIONS I WILL TAKE	BY WHEN
1.			
2.			
3.			

Fig 22. My Goals for Utter Confidence

Practice makes you proficient

Now you've identified your top three priority behaviours, select the first one, identify your goal and then practise, practise, practise. Neurons that fire together, wire together. And so a new behavioural habit is born.

Sharing your goal with a colleague is a good way to get encouragement and support, increasing your chance of following through. Ask people for feedback. Reflect on what you've done differently and the impact that has had.

Reflecting

When you use Behaviour Analysis it's important to reflect on what is working so you increase your chances of repeating the behaviour automatically next time. You can reflect on your behaviours by asking questions like:

"What worked?"

"What was the impact?"

"How did that help?"

There will be times when you'll make mistakes or where the effect you'd intended your chosen behaviour to have isn't achieved. Resist the temptation to say: "Oh I can't do this" or "I give up". No one ever got good at anything without practice. Use these less than perfect situations as opportunities for learning. Questions like these can help you reflect:

"What happened there?"

"What could I have done differently?"

"Which behaviour might have served me better in that interaction?"

Repeat the cycle

As you develop your first behavioural priority, growing in confidence and competence, move onto the second and repeat the 'Practice,

Feedback, Reflect' process. And then onto the third priority. And on it goes.

Experimenting with your team

You may find you want to extend your knowledge of Behaviour Analysis to your team and find the opportunities to play with the different behaviour categories. Appendix C provides you with a number of ways to use elements of the 15 category model to raise awareness and influence behaviours for the better.

2. Behaviour Analysis coaching

Over the years, Behavioural Analysts have worked as coaches to hundred of teams. As part of their work, they:

- Observe interactions

- Collect data – quantitative Behaviour Analysis data and qualitative assessments by the people involved

- Share the data – collectively and individually

- Coach the team on the behavioural priorities for development

This work is sometimes done as a discrete intervention with a team or group that could be working better. Or it could be done in support of other business interactions, such as commercial negotiations and sales coaching. The coaches also use their Behaviour Analysis expertise as part of learning and development programmes for a range of audiences, including leaders, managers, project teams, functional and cross-functional teams.

Here are two examples of team-based coaching to illustrate how Behaviour Analysis can be used. The first case study focuses on a group of engineers, the second on a group of participants in a three-day team leadership event.

Case study 1

I was asked to work with a team of engineers in a utilities business. The guys worked in an environment where the work was complicated and often high risk. The manager was concerned about the team dynamics and how little the team members cooperated with one another. Most of the team were reserved and preferred to work in isolation. However, two team members were more forthcoming, even challenging, in their behaviour.

It was clear that this wasn't an environment where more traditional team coaching was going to work. The engineers were very sceptical of what they called the 'touchy, feely stuff'. We concluded that Behaviour Analysis would be a more appropriate learning vehicle because of its research-base and objectivity.

I first met the team when I went to observe their monthly team meeting. It provided plenty of opportunity to collect data as I saw them in action.

In the second session I gave the team a brief introduction to Behaviour Analysis so that they could understand the basis on which I was working. I then shared the data I had collected from the session and invited the team to work with me to understand what this meant.

The engineers quickly saw some of the obvious messages from the data:

- The airtime was dominated by two people

- One person made very few contributions

- One of the team had a disproportionately high level of

Disagreeing

- Another was 'top of the pops' for Shutting Out
- The level of Seeking Information was very low

From the safety of the objective data we were able to explore the impact of these behaviours and identify what some behavioural alternatives might be.

Each of the team members also benefitted from 1:1 coaching to identify ways in which they might build their behavioural style to the benefit of everyone, so that their own performance could be improved along with that of the team.

Each one of the engineers set a personal behavioural goal that he shared with the team. Over the next few months I made intermittent visits to the team to check their progress. Both the objective data I subsequently collected and the subjective opinion of the team members was evidence that this was now a team that worked in a much more collaborative way. Examples included a member of the team, previously viewed as an 'outsider', being invited into discussions more frequently, and another who made huge progress in managing his frustrations more constructively. Change was effected by holding up a mirror to reflect their behaviours. The rigour and objectivity of Behaviour Analysis overcame their scepticism and became a powerful lever in their on-going development and effectiveness.

Case study 2

As part of a team of three behaviour analysts, I work with a global food manufacturer on their team leadership programme. The three-day event was originally conceived by IMD (Institute of Management Development, Lausanne), and Behaviour Analysis was included in that initial design because of the impact it had had on another of

IMD's clients.

The programme is designed like a mini MBA. Working in teams, participants explore specific topics such as finance and project management. The behaviour analysts accompany the teams through their learning, one analyst per team of 6-8 participants. They collect data over the three days as the team works together on exercises. At four points during the programme they intervene to provide a basic understanding in Behaviour Analysis and provide feedback to the team.

Early intervention helps the teams learn fast: they quickly understand what they can do to perform more effectively (I personally believe that it's more important to help people succeed early than to learn from failure later). The nature of the feedback is different for each group and for each person because the data is unique to that context and those people.

On the final day each participant receives a PBR – a Personal Behaviour Record – that shows his/her behaviour over the course of the event. The observations are often in excess of 5+ hours, yielding a substantial amount of data over the three-day period. Here is a reduced version of a PBR for illustrative purposes:

OBSERVATION SHEET: KLARA BALLI

	BEHAVIOUR	Idea Generation	Milestone Planning	Stakeholder Planning	TOTAL	%
INITIATING	Proposing Procedure		6	6	12	10.4
	Questions and Guidelines: How much are you contributing to providing structure and direction to meetings? Could you have done more?					
	Proposing Content	3		2	5	4.3
	Questions and Guidelines: What is the relationship between your Proposing Content and Building scores? High PC:B suggests more interest in your own ideas, Low PC:B suggests more interest in others' ideas					
	Building			1	1	0.8
	Questions and Guidelines: Low levels of Building will suggest that you are not interested in developing other people's ideas.					
	Seeking Proposals		6	4	10	8.6
	Questions and Guidelines: The higher you score on Seeking Proposals the more you are involving others and demonstrating an interest in their ideas					
REACTING	Supporting	2	3	3	8	7
	Questions and Guidelines: What is your overall level of Reacting? - 10% S + D = Low Reactor, + 20% = High Reactor					
	Disagreeing	6	3	2	11	9.6
	Questions and Guidelines: What is your balance of S : D? High D : Low S = negative impact, Low D : High S dilutes value of S					
	Defend-Attacking					
	Questions and Guidelines: Were you aware of your D-A behaviour? If you used D-A - what effect did you have?					
	Giving Feelings			1	1	0.8
	Questions and Guidelines: Useful for creating openness and a positive climate in meetings. How have you used this behaviour and with what impact?					
	Open		1		1	0.8
	Questions and Guidelines: A way to demonstrate humility. What opportunites did you have?					
	Giving Information	20	5	17	42	36.5
	Questions and Guidelines: GI : SI + TU ratio of + 4 : 1 will suggest that you are mainly interested in your own thoughts and opinions					
	Seeking Information		9	4	13	11.3
	Questions and Guidelines: GI : SI + TU ratio of - 2 : 1 will suggest that you are interested in other people's views as well as your own					
	Testing Understanding		6	1	7	6.1
	Questions and Guidelines: If group has less than 10% TU + SUMM there is risk that meetings lack clear understanding of issues and actions					
	Summarising		3	2	5	4.3
	Questions and Guidelines: How much did you do or did you leave it to others? Practise summarising if you want to develop your listening skills					
	TOTAL	**31**	**42**	**43**	**116**	
PROCESS	Shutting Out	3	4	4	10	8.6
	Questions and Guidelines: Are you getting the airtime you need? Less than 6% of total contributions too low, more than 20% too high					
	Bringing In					
	Questions and Guidelines: Were there times when you could have used BI to involve people more in the meetings?					

Fig 23. Personal Behaviour Record

The PBR is then used in a 1:1 coaching session, where the behaviour analyst works with the individual to understand:

- How representative is this of how you show up at work?
- What might be the impact of some of these behaviours?
- Where are you strong?
- Which behaviours, given the nature of your work, would you most benefit from developing?

As with any training programme, there's a 'window of opportunity' effect: a short period of time after the event for a participant to leverage the value from the training and for the learning to stick. In Papua New Guinea they have an apposite saying for this:

"*Knowledge is only rumour, until it's in the muscle.*" Hence the analysts help participants to shape SMART goals and to support each other in applying their behavioural learning.

This programme is entering its 13th year (mid-2016) and, whilst the design of the programme has changed considerably, Behaviour Analysis remains an integral part. Furthermore, the Behaviour Analysis element consistently ranks as one of the top three top-scoring sessions. That's quite an achievement in a global business where participants hail, on average, from 10 different nations and are often working in English as a second (or third) language.

Concluding remarks

By reading *Master Communication@Work* you now know about the simplicity – and effectiveness – of Behaviour Analysis. As one client remarked: *"This tool is rich with simple ideas that have the potential to make a big impact."*

The stories you've been reading are testimony to that impact and the success it fosters. In each chapter you have also been learning practical behavioural strategies to apply in your daily interactions. Now is your opportunity to have some fun by experimenting with Behaviour Analysis for yourself. Perhaps you have read something that's inspired you or you want to play with some of the suggestions provided in the appendices. In the process of trying out Behaviour Analysis you'll see some immediate results. And, in common with anyone who wants to improve their skills, you will also falter at times. That's par for the course and is, incidentally, more valuable for learning. As Albert Einstein said: *"A person who never made a mistake never tried anything new."*

So, play on, keep going, and you will be successful. If you have any questions or would like to share your experiences, please get in touch. One thing's for sure – your interactions at work will never be the same again!

www.allyyates.com

References

Chapter 1

Collaborative Overload, Cross, R., Rebele, R., Grant, A., Harvard Business Review, Jan-Feb 2016

The Wisdom of Crowds: Why the Many Are Smarter Than the Few, Surowiecki, J., Abacus, 2005

Behaviour Analysis in Training, Rackham, N. and Morgan, T., McGraw-Hill, 1976

The Power of Talk: Who Gets Heard and Why, Tannen, D., Harvard Business Review, Sept-Oct 1995

Talking from 9 to 5: Women and Men at Work: Language, Sex and Power, Tannen, D., Virago, 1996

Developing Interactive Skills, Rackham, N., Honey, P. and Colbert, M., Wellens, 1971

Chapter 2

Four Stages for Learning, Burch, N., Gordon Training International, 1974

Chapter 3

Antagonistic Neural Networks Underlying Differentiated Leadership Roles, Boyatzis, R., Rochford, K. and Jack, A., Frontiers in Human Neuroscience, March 2014

Six Thinking Hats, de Bono, E., Little, Brown and Company, 1985

Facilitating at a Glance: Your Pocket Guide to Facilitation, Bens, I., Goal/QPC, May 2012

Behaviour Analysis in Training, Rackham, N. and Morgan, T., McGraw-Hill, 1976

Media Multitasking and Failures of Attention In Everyday Life, Ralph, B., Thomson, D., Allan Cheyne, J. and Smilek, D., Psychological Research, November 2013

Cognitive Control in Media Multitaskers, Ophir, E., Nass, C., Wagner, A., Proceedings of the National Academy of Sciences, 2009, 106

Chapter 4

Coaching, Mentoring and Organisational Consultancy: Supervision, Skills and Development, Hawkins, P. and Smith, N., Open University Press, 2013

Act Like a Leader, Think Like a Leader, Ibarra, H., Harvard Business Review Press, 2015

Thinking Fast and Slow, Kahneman, D., Allen Lane 2011

What Google Learned From Its Quest to Build the Perfect Team, Duhigg, C., The New York Times, 28 Feb 2016

Team Management: Practical New Approaches, Margerison, C. and McCann, D., Mercury Books, 1995

The Effective Negotiator – Part I: The Behaviour of Successful Negotiators, Rackham, N. & Carlisle, J., Journal of European Industrial Training, Vol. 2, 1978

Chapter 5

Effect Of Colors: Blue Boosts Creativity, While Red Enhances Attention To Detail, Zhu et al, Science Daily, 6 February 2009.

Flow and the Foundations of Positive Psychology, Csikszentihalyi, M., Springer, 2014

The Medici Effect, Johansson, F., Harvard Business Review School Press, 2006

Brainswarming: Because Brainstorming Doesn't Work, McCaffrey, Dr T., Harvard Business Review, March 2014

Behaviour Analysis in Training, Rackham, N. and Morgan, T., McGraw-Hill, 1976

Chapter 6

Behaviour Analysis in Training, Rackham, N. and Morgan, T., McGraw-Hill, 1976

Cultures and Organizations: Software of the Mind, Hofstede, G., Third Edition, McGraw-Hill, 2010

Culture's Consequences: Comparing Values, Behaviours, Institutions and Organizations Across Nations, Hofstede, G., Second Edition, Sage, 2003

Chapter 7

Emotion and the Art of Negotiation, Wood Brooks, A., Harvard Business Review, Dec 2015

Manage Your Emotional Culture, Barsade, S. and O'Neill, O., Harvard Business Review, Jan-Feb 2016

Global Teams That Work, Neeley, T., Harvard Business Review, October 2015

What Google Learned From Its Quest to Build the Perfect Team, Duhigg, C., The New York Times, 28 Feb 2016

Beyond Culture, Hall, Edward T., Anchor Books, 1997

The Effective Negotiator – Part I: The Behaviour of Successful Negotiators, Rackham, N. & Carlisle, J., Journal of European Industrial Training, Vol. 2, 1978

Communication and Trust in Global Virtual Teams, Jarvenpaa, S. and Leidner, D. Organization Science, Dec 1999

Building Trust in High Performing Teams, Hakanen, M. and Soudunsari, A. Technology Innovation Management Review, June 2012

Good to Great, Collins, J., Random House Business, 2001

Talking from 9-5: Men and Women at Work: Language, Sex and Power, Tannen, D., Virago 1996

Resilience: A Practical Guide for Coaches, Pemberton, C., McGraw-Hill Education, 2015

Chapter 8

Consequences for Managers of Using Single Influence Tactics and Combinations of Tactics, Falbe, C. and Yukl, G., Academy of Management Journal, 1992, Volume 35

Personal Power and Influence in Organization Development, Harrison, R., The Collected Papers of Roger Harrison, McGraw-Hill, 1995

Touchpoint Leadership: Creating Collaborative Energy Across Teams and Organizations, Lines, H. and Scholes-Rhodes, J., Kogan Page, 2013

Chapter 9

The Secrets of Great Teamwork, Haas, M. and Mortensen, M., Harvard Business Review, June 2016

Communication and Trust in Global Virtual Teams, Jarvenpaa, S. and Leidner, D., Organization Science, Dec 1999

Power and Trust in Global Virtual Teams, Panteli, N. and Tucker, R., Communications of the ACM, Dec 2009

Team Management: Practical New Approaches, Margerison, C. and McCann, D., Mercury Books, 1995

Quiet: The Power of Introverts in a World That Can't Stop Talking, Cain, S., Viking, 2012

Appendix A: 15 Categories, Definitions and Examples

Here are further examples of each of the behaviour categories to help you to distinguish between them:

BEHAVIOUR	DEFINITION	EXAMPLES
Proposing Procedure	Suggesting of a new course of action, relating to the way in which a pair or group is working -- or could work. (Can be in the form of a statement or a question.)	"Let's move on to talk about pensions." "Please can you take notes?" * "Shall we take a break?" "Over to you Richard…"
Proposing Content	Suggesting a new concept or idea which is actionable, which relates to the topic being discussed	"Why don't we advertise for candidates?" ** "I suggest we use head-hunters." "We could use our networks to identify suitable candidates." ***
Building	Extending or developing a proposal already made by another person	"And could you use the flip chart to capture the key points please?" * "If I could add to that and suggest we do online advertising as well as the trade journals." ** "Yes, LinkedIn would be an excellent way of doing that." *** "I think that idea would work if we got everyone involved."
Seeking Proposals	Directly asking another, or others, for a proposal or build	"Who would like to start?" "What ideas do you have?" "How should we do this?" "Who needs to be involved?" "When can you do it?"
Supporting	Making a clear statement of agreement with, or support for, a person or their statement, opinion, idea or approach	"Yes. I think that's right." "Sounds good to me." "OK then, let's do it." "Well done, you have done a great job." "Rose is right."
Disagreeing	Making a clear statement of disagreement with someone else's statement, opinion, idea or approach, or raising objections to such a contribution	"That won't work for me." "What you are saying just isn't right." "I can't agree with you." "I don't like that idea." "I think that's wrong."
Defending-Attacking	Attacking another person (as distinct from an issue) directly, or defending yourself against such attacks. Such behaviour is usually judgmental and emotional	"You're being ridiculous." "Don't look at me – it's not my fault." "You guys are as slow as a tortoise." "Gosh Susan, I think you're on another planet." "Trust an accountant to see things differently."
Giving Feelings	An expression of your feelings about the current situation or work in progress	"I'm uncomfortable about that last point." "I'm much happier now you've explained it further." "There's something about this that doesn't feel quite right." "I'm really pleased with the progress we're making." "I'm shocked!" "I'm getting bored with this."

BEHAVIOUR	DEFINITION	EXAMPLES
Open	Non-defensive admissions of mistakes or inadequacies	"My apologies, I completely forgot about it." "Whoops! My mistake." "I don't think I had prepared enough." "It may be my fault." "I should have thought of that earlier."
Giving Information	Making a statement of fact, opinion or reason to another person(s)	"We have two vacancies at the moment." "The project is moving into the final stage." "I think that this is a great opportunity for expansion." "This is the better of the two handsets." "My view is that Peter is the best man for the job."
Seeking Information	Seeking facts, opinions or reasons from other(s)	"Who is involved?" "Where are we on budget?" "Why is this one better?" "How did the client react?" "What happened?" "What's the purpose of the meeting?"
Testing Understanding	Checking out an assumption or checking whether a previous contribution has been correctly understood	"Can I just check we're talking about the same person?" "Does that mean you want to recruit more than two people?" "Are you saying she's not up to the job?" "You're going on Monday, is that right?"
Summarising	Repeating, accurately and in a condensed form (with nothing new) the content of all or part of the preceding discussion	"Clare will look at risk management, Chris will focus on stakeholder management and Jane will focus on the budget?" "Clare and Chris agree but it seems Jane is uncertain." "So we won't advertise. Instead we'll use a head-hunter and reach out to our networks, including LinkedIn."
Shutting Out	Behaving in a way that prevents or shortens another's contribution - most typically, cutting across a speaker by interrupting and/or answering a question posed to someone else	Clare: "What do you think Chris?" Jane: "I'm happy." (Jane is Shutting Out by answering a question intended for Chris.) Clare: "I think I could do that because…" Alyse (Shutting Out by interrupting): "Yes, I think you could."
Bringing In	Seeking a contribution from a person who has not contributed for some time or at all	"Chris, is there anything you'd like to say?" "Alyse, you've not had a chance to say anything, what do you think?" "Tom, I notice you've been rather quiet – what are you thinking?"

NB: The number of asterisks in the Proposing behaviours and Building

Fig 24. a and b – Categories, Definitions and Examples

Appendix B: Behaviour Analysis Ready Reminder

This page is designed to be a helpful reminder for your interactions. It's also available to download from **www.allyyates.com**

	BEHAVIOUR	GUIDELINES
INITIATING	Proposing Procedure	How much are you contributing to providing structure and direction? Could you have done more?
	Proposing Content	What is the relationship between your Proposing Content and Building scores?
	Building	How interested are you in developing other people's ideas?
	Seeking Proposals	Are you inviting ideas from others?
REACTING	Supporting	How often did you take the opportunity to support a contribution or a person?
	Disagreeing	Were you able to voice your disagreements without labelling?
	Defend-Attacking	What effect is this having?
EXPRESSING	Giving Feelings	Useful for creating openness and a positive climate in meetings
	Open	A way to demonstrate humility
CLARIFYING	Giving Information	Giving : Seeking + Testing Understanding ratio
	Seeking Information	How varied are your questions?
	Testing Understanding	How often did you clarify information for yourself and others?
	Summarising	How much did you do or did you leave it to others? Practise summarising if you want to develop your listening skills
PROCESS	Shutting Out	Has everyone had the chance to contribute?
	Bringing In	Do you need others to contribute more?
	Labelling	Helpful to get airtime and attention - 1. A non verbal signal 2. Behaviour Labelling 3. Category of behaviour

Fig 25. Behaviour Analysis Ready Reminder

Appendix C: Using Behaviour Analysis with your Team

There are lots of ways you can begin to use Behaviour Analysis in your interactions and some of the easiest ways to start to experiment are listed below.

It's unlikely that someone new to Behaviour Analysis can accurately record all 15 categories. Therefore it's useful to begin by capturing just one or two.

The Fifteen Second Rule

In capturing data we use something called 'The Fifteen Second Rule'. This means that if anyone talks for more than 15 seconds, another mark is made for that category. For example, if you talk for a minute describing how you have dealt with a situation at work, this would be 4 contributions marked in the Giving Information category.

Here are the top ten suggestions for how you can begin to capture data and then use this with your colleagues as the basis for discussion to identify strengths and areas for improvement. On the website: **www.allyyates.com** you will find observation forms to use for each of these, along with further explanation.

1. **Airtime**

Collect the total number of contributions per person, without differentiating between categories

NAME	CONTRIBUTIONS	TOTAL
Felix	卌 卌 卌 卌 卌 卌 卌 II	37
Sue	卌 卌 II	12
Joanna	卌 卌 卌 III	18
Warwick	卌 卌 卌 I	16
Simon	卌 III	8

Total number of contributions per person in descending order				
Felix: 37	Joanna: 18	Warwick: 16	Sue: 12	Simon: 8
RATIO HIGHEST:LOWEST CONTRIBUTOR = 4.6 : 1				

Fig 26. Capturing Airtime

2. Participation

Collect the total number of contributions plus Shutting Out and Bringing In for each person

3. Clarity

Collect the total number of contributions plus Testing Understanding and Summarising for each person

4. Structure

Collect the total number of contributions plus Proposing Procedure by person

5. Ideas (1)

Collect the total number of contributions plus Proposing Content and Seeking Proposals by person

6. **Interest in others**

Collect the total number of contributions plus Seeking Proposals and Seeking Information by person

7. **Reacting**

Collect the total number of contributions plus Supporting and Disagreeing by person

8. **Expressing**

Collect the total number of contributions plus Giving Feelings and Open by person

9. **Ideas (2)**

Collect the total number of contributions plus Proposing Content and Building by person

10. **Cluster balance**

Collect the total number of contributions by cluster (Initiating, Reacting, Expressing, Clarifying, Process)

About the Author

Ally combines expertise in people and business. She works with clients to build insights, to develop capability and to deliver results.

Her corporate career started with an international consultancy specialising in sales and people management skills, and then to Coopers & Lybrand where she re-engineered the firm's business development process and set up a centre of excellence for major bids. She subsequently took on the role of director in the PricewaterhouseCoopers Strategy practice, including the management of 120 staff.

Her success in the corporate arena draws on her earlier career as a therapist (understanding people) and then a researcher (looking for evidence) and further developed as she gained consultancy experience (valuing diversity). Her expertise lies in change management, business development, leadership, performance development/management, team development and coaching. She is a leader in the field of behaviour analysis.

Since 2000 Ally has been working as an independent consultant, facilitator, trainer and coach, working with managers and leaders across industry sectors and across geographies.

Ally is passionate about rugby. She loves travel, reading, singing and learning. Her biggest joy is her family.

JAICO PUBLISHING HOUSE
Elevate Your Life. Transform Your World.

ESTABLISHED IN 1946, Jaico Publishing House is home to world-transforming authors such as Sri Sri Paramahansa Yogananda, Osho, The Dalai Lama, Sri Sri Ravi Shankar, Sadhguru, Robin Sharma, Deepak Chopra, Jack Canfield, Eknath Easwaran, Devdutt Pattanaik, Khushwant Singh, John Maxwell, Brian Tracy and Stephen Hawking.

Our late founder Mr. Jaman Shah first established Jaico as a book distribution company. Sensing that independence was around the corner, he aptly named his company Jaico ('Jai' means victory in Hindi). In order to service the significant demand for affordable books in a developing nation, Mr. Shah initiated Jaico's own publications. Jaico was India's first publisher of paperback books in the English language.

While self-help, religion and philosophy, mind/body/spirit, and business titles form the cornerstone of our non-fiction list, we publish an exciting range of travel, current affairs, biography, and popular science books as well. Our renewed focus on popular fiction is evident in our new titles by a host of fresh young talent from India and abroad. Jaico's recently established Translations Division translates selected English content into nine regional languages.

In addition to being a publisher and distributor of its own titles, Jaico is a major national distributor of books of leading international and Indian publishers. With its headquarters in Mumbai, Jaico has branches and sales offices in Ahmedabad, Bangalore, Bhopal, Bhubaneswar, Chennai, Delhi, Hyderabad, Kolkata and Lucknow.

SINCE 1946